from Ruth

Restoring furnishings for the home

Consultant Editor Ann Lamacraft

RESTORING
furnishings for the home

B. T. BATSFORD LTD., LONDON

Acknowledgements:
Consultant editor: Ann Lamacraft
Illustrations by Alan Young for
Alias Design, London
Design by Clive Sutherland

The publishers also wish to thank
Carolyn Chapman, Sonya Mills, Hilary
Moore, Helen Morse, Arthur Nicklin
and Alan Taylor for their contributions
to the manuscript. They also thank
Isabel Clark and Sarah Dacey for their
help and support.

Text and illustrations © Ventura
Publishing Ltd., 1982
First published in Great Britain in
1982 by B. T. Batsford Limited,
4 Fitzhardinge Street,
London W1H 0AH

Created and produced by Ventura
Publishing Ltd., 44 Uxbridge Street,
London W8 7TG

ISBN 0 7134 4025 2

Filmset by SX Composing Ltd.,
Rayleigh, Essex
Colour origination by D. S. Colour
International Limited, London
Printed in Spain by
Editorial Fher 3A, Bilbao

Other titles in the series
By Heinz and Geneste Kurth
BARBEQUE and the joy of cooking
on an open fire
GREENHOUSES for longer summers
OUTDOOR HOLIDAYS for indoor
people
WINEMAKING at home

Contents

Wood 7

Caning and upholstery 29

Textiles and fabrics 41

Chinaware and glassware 51

Metals 61

Pictures, prints and frames 69

Stonework 73

Glossary 77

List of suppliers 78

Index 80

Restoring furniture involves three quite separate operations: cleaning, refinishing and repairing, plus, quite often, undoing the work of a previous 'restorer' – for example replacing inappropriate handles. But a good restorer does only the minimum work necessary. The wood must be clean, but not over-cleaned so that the patina, the subtle gloss built up over the years, disappears. It should shine, but not with such a high gloss that it looks factory-fresh. Broken parts must be repaired so that the piece functions as intended, but a few dents, scars and cracks are acceptable signs of age. New fittings should resemble the originals as closely as possible.

Household treasures made of wood are usually items of furniture: tables, chairs and all kinds of cabinets. Such things are strongly made, and last for hundreds of years; but during their long lives they take a terrible beating and it does not take many years to turn a nice piece of furniture into a wreck. Fortunately most of the damage is quite easy to put right, given a little know-how, a few basic tools and, most important of all, plenty of patience.

ESSENTIAL TOOLS
These are all basic hand tools which will also be needed for general household maintenance and repair.

Screwdrivers, large and small
Hammer, tack hammer
Saws, tenon and panel saw, coping saw for curved cutting
Steel straight edge or ruler
Knives, trimming, craft, scalpel, stripping and filling
Files, rasp or wood
Scrapers, patent types and razor blade in holder
Shave hooks
Pincers, pliers, tack lifter

G-clamps (pair)
Hand drill (wheelbrace) and twist drills
Junior hacksaw
Bradawl
Nail punch
Cork sanding block, patent sanding tools
Paint brushes, decorator's and artist's

ADDITIONAL TOOLS
Power tool with range of sanding attachments
Vice (can be portable if you have no work bench)
Chisels, several sizes of general-purpose type
Mallet
Plane
Combination square or try-square
Brace and large wood drilling bits
Spokeshave
Mitre box

SIZING UP THE WORK
Whatever type of furniture you intend to restore do not rush into action without studying it closely first. If you are buying the piece secondhand, it is important to check for structural damage to make sure you do not buy something which needs skilled repair work calling for specialised tools. Tilt chairs back and press down on the seat to find out if joints are just loose, or actually broken. Bounce on sprung seats to feel if any of the coils are loose. Test all moving parts such as doors, drawers and table leaves. Look for woodworm damage hiding in the back and underside. Check that there are no pieces missing altogether, such as chair rails, a plinth front or a cornice moulding. They may be around somewhere, or if not you could get the price reduced because of the defect. Assess whether damage to any decorative work such as moulding, carving or inlay work can be repaired or is liveable with.

Before starting remove all knobs, handles etc. This makes the basic piece easier to work on, protects the fittings from damage and enables them to be thoroughly cleaned separately. Tackle any major repair work first. Unless it is obvious that complete stripping is necessary, give the piece a good clean up. This will reveal any minor repairs that need doing, such as removing surface blemishes, and indicate whether the finish needs reviving or renewing. Make any repairs to veneers or inlays before stripping with chemicals, to prevent it getting underneath and causing more trouble.

CLEANING CLEAR-FINISHED FURNITURE

However dirt- and wax-encrusted the wood may be do not be tempted to use harsh cleaning methods. Hot water, detergent, scouring powder and scrubbing brushes are out, as they would ruin the finish. Hot water can also raise the grain of the wood, loosen joints and lift veneers. What is needed is a solvent which will remove the wax, taking the dirt with it. You can make your own with four parts of white spirit to one of linseed oil, or buy a proprietary restorer and cleaner, which is based on refined alcohol and turpentine, and has a stronger action.

The white spirit mixture, rubbed on with a coarse cloth pad, will only remove dirt and wax, and will not touch a French polish or other finish underneath. Keep turning the pad as you work to expose a clean

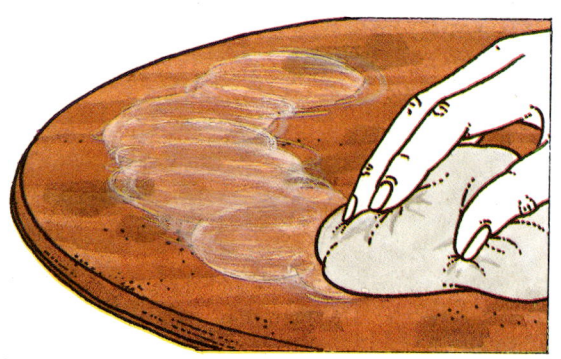

surface. If this method does not seem to be making much impression, or you need to get into fancy mouldings or carving, use fine steel wool (grade oo) but only rub lightly or the finish may start to come off as well. The proprietary restorer and cleaner, used with fine steel wool, dissolves the top layer of a French polish finish as well as dirt and wax. If rubbed on gently with a cloth it just takes off the latter.

Cleaning should not be overdone – the colour change around moulding and carving caused by ingrained dirt is one of the things that give old furniture its unique character.

Once dirt/wax/surface finish have been removed go over the piece again with clean solvent to make sure that every trace of it has been removed and that there are no overlap marks.

CLEANING PAINTED FURNITURE

A painted item which you intend to repaint can be cleaned with warm water and detergent, or a proprietary paint cleaner, which is mildly abrasive and does not foam up. Rinse off with plain water and wipe the piece thoroughly dry afterwards so that no water gets into joints or under the paint film. If furniture is to be stripped there is no point in cleaning it first unless the dirt is so thick and greasy it would inhibit the stripper.

Furniture with decorative painting on it, as opposed to ordinary one- or two-colour work, needs very gentle cleaning to avoid rubbing off the motifs. Warm water and detergent, sparingly used, should be all right, but test it on a small patch to check for any sign of discoloration. Do not use anything abrasive.

CLEANING FITTINGS

Strip paint from knobs, handles etc., by steeping them in chemical stripper poured into a small container. Clean badly corroded metal with fine steel wool; a toothbrush is useful for ornate brass handles. Finish off with metal polish. China knobs should only need washing, but tired-looking white ones can benefit from a soak in bleach (not if painted or gold lined).

REVIVING AND POLISHING

If cleaning has revealed any surface defects, treat these now as described overleaf. If the finish appears sound, but looks dull and lifeless, it needs further treatment called reviving, which can be done in a variety of ways.

One method is to polish it with a gentle liquid abrasive, i.e., metal polish, car paint cleaner or a proprietary burnishing cream. Alternatively, on a French polished surface you can rub in boiled linseed oil, or a wood reviver based on this. Leave these to soak in and dry for at least 24 hours before polishing.

Another method of reviving is to apply a new coat of the original finish, which means finding out what this was (although a reviving coat of French polish can be used over anything). To test for French polish rub the surface with a rag dipped in methylated spirit to see if it starts to dissolve. Cellulose lacquer will dissolve if rubbed with cellulose thinners; modern polyurethane varnish will remain untouched by either.

Before applying a fresh coat of polyurethane varnish rub the surface lightly with fine abrasive paper to give it grip. Cellulose is a factory finish which was sprayed on, and there is no particular point in re-applying it, even if you had access to the equipment and the varnish, as polyurethane gives the same gloss but is far more durable. Fresh cellulose and polyurethane varnishes do not mix happily together, but you should not have any trouble with an old, hard cellulose finish provided it is well rubbed down before applying the polyurethane.

Some furniture, particularly teak, has none of these finishes but has simply been oiled. This soaks into the grain of the wood and enriches the colour, giving only a slight sheen. Revival is simply a matter of rubbing in two or three fresh coats.

Good-quality country furniture, such as elm and yew chairs, may have a waxed finish, and can be

revived by polishing alone. If dirt has penetrated the old wax, giving the piece a greyish look, remove it first with steel wool and white spirit.

After carrying out any of the above reviving treatments (except oiling) give the piece a final burnishing with a good-quality wax polish. Most are clear, but if you want to deepen the colour of the wood some are available in tinted form, suitable for light, medium and dark woods. Very dark ones are sometimes called antique waxes.

BLEMISHES

Most old furniture will have acquired at least a few blemishes over the years. The most common ones are scratches; marks caused by water, heat or alcohol; and stains such as ink. How easy they are to remove depends very much on whether they have only penetrated the finish, or reached the wood itself. It is always worth trying some of the more gentle methods outlined below first. They can be remarkably successful, and only if they fail should you resort to stronger methods which remove all the finish.

Removing a blemish cannot be done without taking some of the finish off too, so you then have to patch it up. If the mark was in the finish only, this is not too difficult. However, if you have had to scrape or sand right down to clean wood, building up a patch of new finish that blends in with the old one calls for quite a lot of skill and not a little luck. It is, therefore, worth trying patch methods first, before going to the laborious length of stripping, sanding and refinishing the whole surface.

If possible use the same material for patching a finish as was used in the first place. A coat or two over the whole surface, once the patch has dried, will help to blend it in.

Disguising scratches Very slight scratches may disappear if rubbed with a fine liquid abrasive such as metal polish, or proprietary scratch remover. Another technique is just to disguise them by applying dark polish (or shoe polish) on scratches that show up light. Otherwise rub them using fine abrasive paper in the direction of the grain.

A craftsman's technique for repairing a fairly deep scratch is to build it up with coats of French polish, left in a saucer for a few minutes so that it thickens slightly. Apply several coats so that the former scratch ends up higher than the surrounding surface, using a fine artist's paint brush to restrict the polish to the damaged area. When the repair is hard scrape it flat with a scalpel blade, rub down with very fine abrasive paper and put on yet another coat of polish. (Remem-

ber when buying the polish that French polish is brown; for pale wood get white polish.) The same technique can be used with varnish, but use it straight from the can.

Disguising burn marks Scrape away the charred wood with a sharp craft knife or scalpel and smooth with fine abrasive paper. Tint if necessary, using artist's oil, wood stains or felt tip pen, and build up any noticeable depression as previously described before refinishing.

Disguising white rings and heat marks If superficial these may yield to rubbing with mild abrasive as for scratches. If the item is French polished try rubbing gently with a soft cloth moistened in methylated spirit. This dissolves the finish, so it must then be built up again.

Disguising dark stains and rings These are usually caused by ink, sometimes red wine, but water penetrating the finish can look similar. Bleaching is the treatment here; but first remove the old finish so that it can penetrate the wood. Use ordinary domestic bleach (the thickened kind is useful as it is easier to confine it to the stained area). Wear gloves and do not breathe in the fumes, which are powerful if the chemical is used neat. Be careful not to get any drops on other parts of the furniture – have a clean rag handy to mop up *immediately*. Dab the bleach on with a rag, wrapped round a stick if the spot is small, and watch carefully so that you can wash it off as soon as the wood has lightened to the tone required. This may take minutes or hours, depending on the intensity of the stain.

Alternatively you can use proprietary wood bleach, which is a two-part product; follow the instructions carefully as it is quite a dangerous substance.

As with a burn, you will probably be left with a pale patch that needs tinting to match the surrounding area before refinishing.

Bleaching may not be a hundred per cent successful if the ink has sunk deep into the grain, but it should reduce the mark to the point where staining the whole item a shade or two darker than before will produce a reasonably even tone overall.

REPAIRING DEEP SCRATCHES, CRACKS AND SPLITS

Any of these can be repaired with filler provided it is deep enough (if too shallow it is very hard not to remove the filler when trying to sand it flat) and has a bottom to it. Modern plastic fillers are so elastic and quick-drying that even bottomless splits can be filled if not too wide.

In most cases the filler to use is wood stopper or plastic wood. The latter is harder and is also good for jobs like building up a damaged moulding or repairing carving. Both are available in a variety of wood shades. The basic technique is to pack the filler hard into the

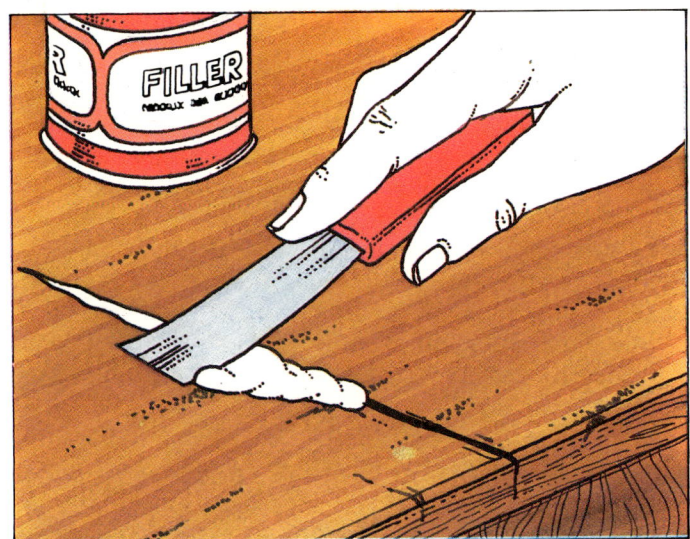

hole with a flexible filling knife, over-filling slightly as it tends to shrink while drying. Work quickly, as plastic wood in particular starts to dry at once, and very quickly becomes unworkable. Allow to dry hard and then sand level before refinishing. Make sure tins and tubes are tightly closed immediately, or the material will go rock hard.

When a piece is going to be repainted the filling can be done with ordinary cellulose filler used for decorating work, which is cheaper if there is a lot to be done, as the white patches will be hidden. A decorator's trick is to mix the filler with a little of the undercoat instead of water, as otherwise filler absorbs more paint than wood does and the filled spots show up less glossy in the finished work.

The very long, wide splits which often occur in the end panels of chests of drawers are traditionally repaired by inserting a tapered lath of matching wood, but this is a highly skilled job. You may be able to do it with filler, if you back the split with some self-adhesive carpet tape.

Gaps around loose-fitting joints *can* be filled, but unless the joint has been repaired in some way they will open up in time.

REPAIRING VENEERS, INLAYS AND MARQUETRY

Veneers are thin sheets of attractive, expensive wood glued on to a groundwork of cheaper wood which forms the carcass of the furniture. Sometimes the veneering consists of plain panels, sometimes the panels are inlaid with other woods, or occasionally more exotic substances such as mother of pearl. The words inlay and marquetry are used somewhat interchangeably, and can mean anything from narrow strips or plain or patterned bands let into the main panel, to a series of elaborate marquetry motifs, usually showing flowers, shells and fans.

As veneers are so thin they are prone to various kinds of failure. Movement of the groundwork causes splits; glue dries out and pieces fall off; blisters appear. Making repairs may mean getting hold of some new matching pieces, or whole sheets of veneer.

Blisters These are quite easy to repair. Slit the blister with a sharp craft knife to release trapped air. Soften the veneer with a damp pad and a hot iron. Squeeze in a little adhesive on the point of a knife and press the blister gently down; weight until dry. If the blister is already split open it will have dirt inside. Soften it as before, then ease it open and scrape the inside clean with, say, a large oval nail before gluing and weighting.

Damaged patches When the edge of a panel of veneer has broken away, or a small area is stained or damaged beyond repair, the treatment is to put in a patch. It is important to match the grain and figure of the wood as closely as you can; colour can be adjusted by obtaining a slightly lighter veneer and staining it. To make the patch as inconspicuous as possible it should be triangular or diamond-shaped (Fig 1).

Place a square or rectangle of new veneer over the damage so it overlaps all round, matching the grain, and tape it in place (Fig 2). Cut through both layers with a sharp craft knife held against a steel straight edge (Fig 3). Remove the patch, ease off the damaged veneer and scrape the groundwork clean of old glue. Glue the

patch in place. If it is possible to weight or cramp the patch while the adhesive dries, use ordinary wood-working adhesive. If not use contact adhesive. When the adhesive is completely dry trim off any overhang left on an edge repair (Fig 4). If possible turn the piece upside down so this can be done from underneath. Sand the patch smooth and finish to match the rest.

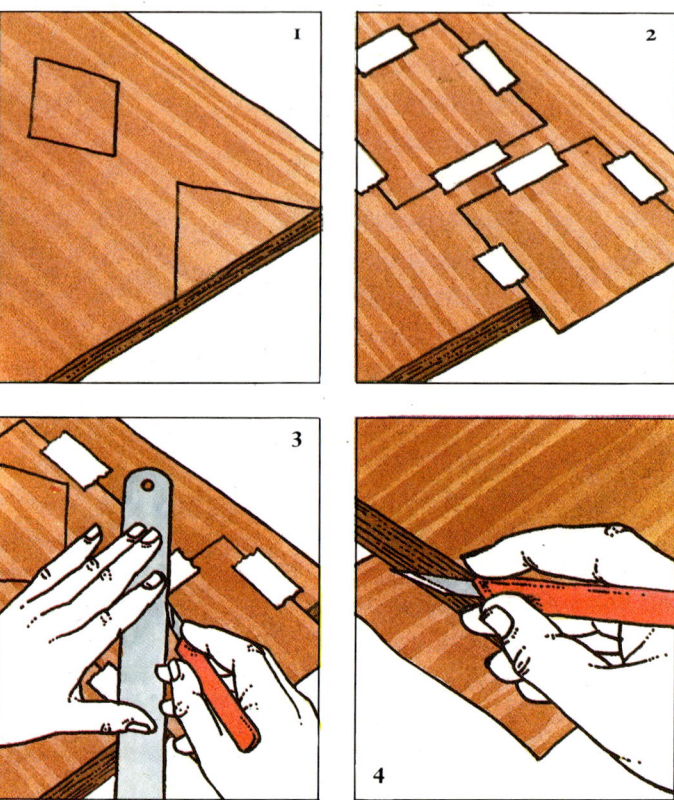

When pieces of inlay work have gone missing, nearby pieces may prove to be almost off, and will have to be lifted and reglued, because there is bound to be dirt underneath. First make a pattern for the missing bits by laying a piece of tracing paper over the spot and rubbing over the edges of the surrounding pieces with a very soft pencil. To get the loose pieces off intact cover them with a damp cloth and leave overnight. Then iron over a damp cloth to soften the glue, and gently lever them off with a thin flat blade. Arrange them in order on a piece of paper on top of a board, cover with paper, weight down and leave to dry for at least a week. Clean the groundwork and proceed as for patching.

Replacing a veneer panel If a complete panel of veneer is hopelessly split, lifting and damaged, replace the whole thing. Steam press it as above to melt the glue, then peel and scrape the old veneer away (keep any sizeable pieces for future repair work). Prepare the groundwork with coarse abrasive paper so that it is clean and flat, but not too smooth; slight roughness gives a key for the adhesive. This can be glue film or contact adhesive. Brush contact adhesive thinly on to both surfaces (Fig 1). Do not use the comb that may be supplied as this gives a thick layer designed for laminated plastic. When it is nearly dry place a piece of brown paper over the groundwork a few inches short of one end (Fig 2). It will not stick but allows you more time to work. Position the veneer, allowing an overlap for trimming on all sides. Gradually pull out the paper and press down the veneer, starting where the paper stops short and working methodically down (Fig 3). It helps to have a second person to withdraw the paper. The proper tool is a veneer hammer but you can use a wallpaper seam roller or a small block of wood. The important thing is to push out all the air underneath so that the veneer is adhering to the groundwork all over, with no missed spots. Trim the edges as for patches (Fig 4).

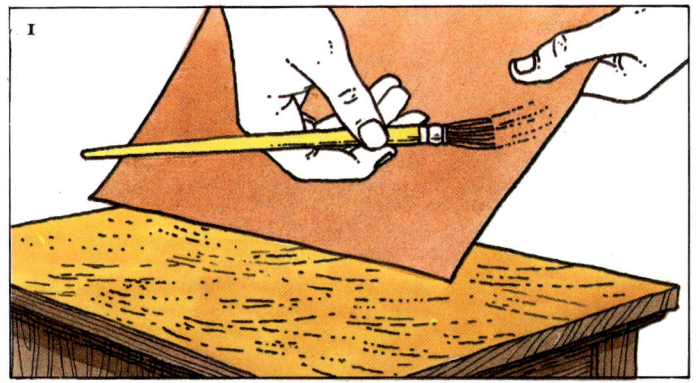

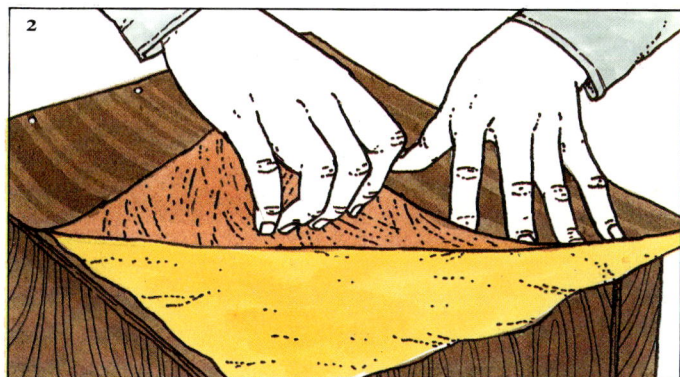

CRAMPING

The basic tool for cramping pieces of wood together while the adhesive dries is a G-clamp (Fig 1). It is always used with pieces of wood between the jaws to protect the furniture from marks. It should not be over-tightened; this can push a repair out of shape, and is unnecessary. Only light pressure is required, but it must be sustained. G-clamps come in a range of sizes, with jaws from 5cm (2in) to 20cm (8in) across. You need at least two, as they often have to be used in pairs. A plain steel right angle cramp is cheaper than the proper G-clamp and adequate for occasional use.

When an item is too big for even the largest G-clamp professional restorers use sash cramps, pairs of adjustable shoes sliding on a long metal bar. These are much too expensive for the occasional job, and the amateur's substitute is some form of tourniquet (Fig 2). This can be used on anything with straight sides, so that a loop of cord can be placed around it without slipping off. After protecting the corners or other spots where the cord touches the wood, to prevent marks, tighten the cord by twisting a stick around it. Make sure when cramping up a drawer, or any kind of frame, that it has not become diamond-shaped, or it will set that way permanently. To check for squareness

measure the diagonals in each direction; they should be exactly the same.

Binding a mend up tightly with strong sticky tape (Fig 3) is another possible method, convenient for splits in small components.

If you have a work bench you can improvise cramping devices with lengths of wood and pairs of wedges, known as folding wedges. A typical arrangement, designed to hold three planks forming a table top while the adhesive sets, could consist of strips screwed to the work bench, parallel and slightly wider apart than the work. The wedges are then tapped in to get an exact fit (not too tight, or the work will lift up off the bench). A vice can be used in a similar way.

Cramping curving parts calls for considerable ingenuity, to devise something that will not slip off the piece in question. A professional restorer will make special blocks of wood for this kind of work, shaped to fit the component and enable a sash cramp or tourniquet to be put on.

When cramping by weight is called for, as when repairing veneer work, any kind of weight can be used, from encyclopedias to buckets of water, stood on a board if necessary to distribute the load.

1 *G clamp*   **2** *tourniquet*   **3** *sticky tape*

14

REPAIRING FAILED JOINTS

These are natural weak spots, found particularly in chairs; the wear and tear of years, plus wood shrinkage and dried-out glue, can make them loosen, so that the furniture wobbles, and eventually breaks apart altogether. The joints used in furniture construction most likely to need mending are mortise and tenons, dowel joints and dovetails. These are all different ways of fitting a protrusion on one part of a piece of furniture into a hole in another.

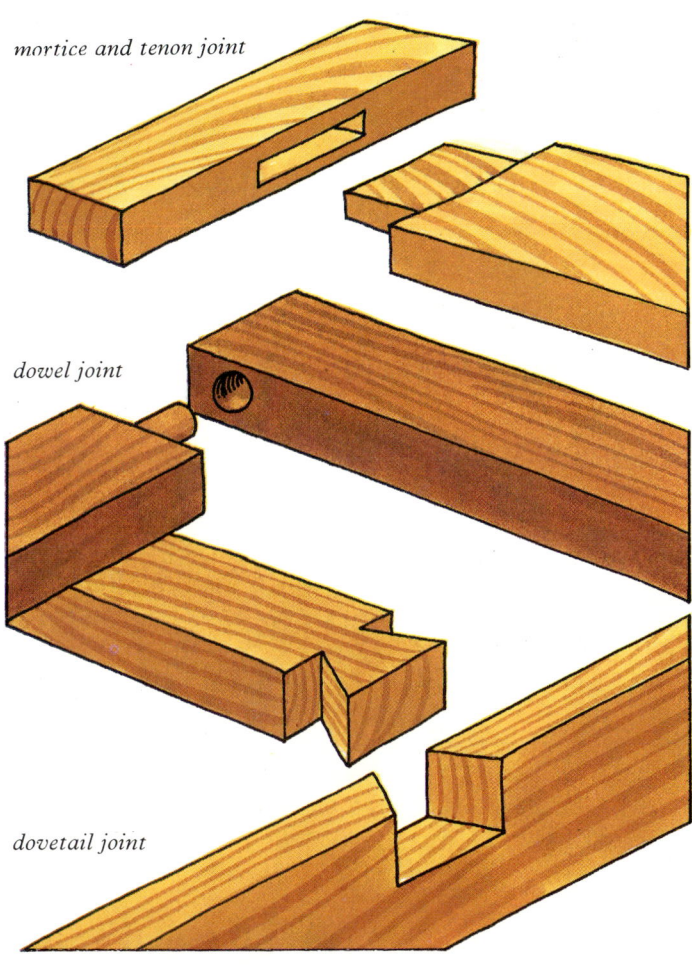

mortice and tenon joint

dowel joint

dovetail joint

To repair a loose joint effectively you have to knock it apart, clean up the surfaces and reglue it. While the glue is drying the joint must be cramped together.

Before starting look for any reinforcing dowels, nails or screws and remove them. If the old Scotch glue is still holding, soften it with hot water or steam. Either dribble boiling water into the joint, or fit a kettle spout with a cork and length of plastic tubing so you can blow a jet of steam into the joint. (Wear gloves as the end of the tube will be hot, and do not let the kettle boil dry.) Knock the joint gently apart with a mallet or hammer, protecting the surface with a scrap of wood. Thoroughly clean all sides of the joint, scraping and sanding off any remaining glue.

If dismantling an item completely, for example a chair, label the pieces so that you can reassemble them in exactly the same order. Put them together dry, without adhesive, to check that everything fits, then glue back together in sections; do not try to do the whole thing at once. Paint each joint all over with woodworking adhesive, cramp up and leave overnight to dry.

Mortise and tenon joints so badly worn that the surfaces are no longer flat will not stick together firmly. Using a gap-filling adhesive may solve the problem, but if not skilled work is called for. Basically what you have to do is cut the surfaces back so they are flat again, then build them up to the required size by gluing on new pieces of hardwood. Rebuilding a broken tenon calls for even more skill than making a new one, so it is not something to try unless you are fairly practised at that.

Repair plates Although no craftsman would dream of using these, mortise and tenons, and other square joints, can be repaired with them provided they can be kept out of sight. If you are not able to make a proper repair, or as a temporary measure, they are better than nothing and will stop the joint from deteriorating still further. Repair plates are made of steel, right-angled, T-shaped or straight. The right-angled ones are good for repairing the joints on a seat

or table frame formerly strengthened by wooden blocks. T-shaped ones are for joining a horizontal section to a vertical one in the same plane. Straight ones can help hold together planks forming a kitchen table that are trying to spring apart.

Dowel joints are easier to repair as the tenon part, the dowel, is a separate piece and can be replaced. Remove the damaged dowel either by pulling it out with pincers, or if it has broken off flush drill the bulk of it out and scrape the rest away. Small dowel joints can be bought ready for use, but large long ones will have to be prepared from an appropriately-sized length of plain hardwood dowel. Cut off a length 1.5mm ($\frac{1}{16}$in) shorter than the combined depth of the two holes; saw a slot down one side to allow excess glue to escape; chamfer each end with a file to help it slide easily into its hole. Spread adhesive over the dowels, assemble the joint, cramp and leave.

Dovetail joints most commonly in need of repair are those joining the four sides of a drawer. To take a drawer apart without wrecking the dovetails, first slide out the bottom panel. Then gently knock the joints apart, following the procedure for mortise and tenon joints. Work on each joint in turn, to loosen them all before finally dismantling the drawer. Cramp and reglue as above; if the dovetails are damaged a few fine panel pins may be necessary. Do not forget to replace the bottom!

SPLITS, BREAKS AND MISSING PARTS

Although wood is a strong material it can split if put under too much strain, or it may snap completely, usually in a vulnerable spot like the thinnest part of a turned chair leg.

General splits and breaks can be glued together very successfully *if* the damage is recent and the pieces match perfectly. An old break will have lost little fragments of wood and gathered dirt which repels adhesives; a split may have hopelessly distorted the wood fibres. Use modern woodworking adhesive (PVA), which is extremely strong and will make a good sound join provided you are able to cramp the repair together while it dries. In the case of chair legs it is wise to add some reinforcement.

Replacements If the broken or missing part is rectangular or round, such as a plain chair rail, replacing it should be no problem. Take the remains of the component, or the measurements of a matching one, to a timber merchant dealing in hardwood and get a new piece of wood. There is unlikely to be anything exactly the same size; get something slightly larger in section to plane and/or rasp down to size.

Turned rails or legs can only be produced on a lathe. Approach any of the following to make what you want: a timber merchant who advertises turning work; someone who does woodturning as a hobby; any local institution that runs classes in wood turning.

Hardwood mouldings can be obtained from specialist suppliers. If you cannot obtain a match, take off nearby mouldings and replace them with the nearest thing available.

Most replacements will need staining to match the rest of the piece. Ideally they should be the same species of wood, but if you are not very sure what this is, or getting hold of it is too difficult, use an anonymous-looking hardwood like ramin.

Broken or missing rails A similar technique can be used for any kind of rail: saw a broken round chair rail off close to both legs. Remove the stubs by drilling into them with a slightly smaller drill – they

1 *Saw the broken round rail off close to the legs.*

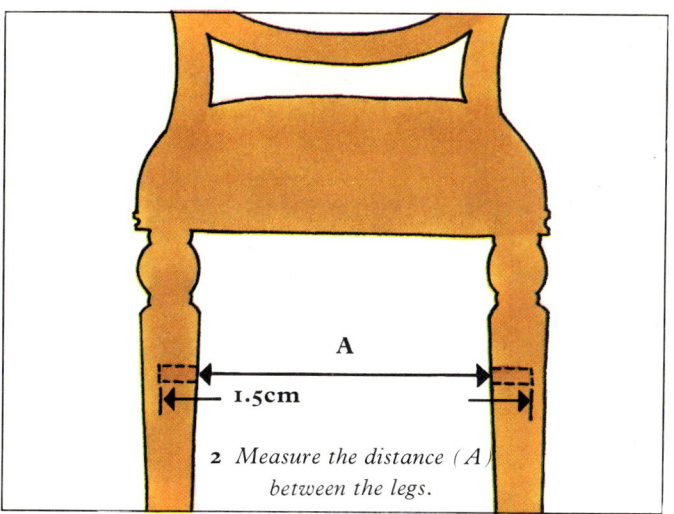

A
1.5cm

2 *Measure the distance (A) between the legs.*

REPLACING HANDLES AND KNOBS

On old furniture the former are usually brass, while the latter can also be wooden or china. If any are missing, replacements should be available from one of the specialist suppliers.

Wooden knobs often break at the base, and provided the piece is still around it can be glued back. Some are fixed by an integral wooden screw; if this has had its thread stripped off, or is broken, repair it by plugging the hole in the drawer with filler and pushing the screw home before it sets; or applying adhesive to the flat back of the knob. (Remove the finish from the drawer in the knob area to give the adhesive grip; do not glue on to veneer as this would have to be cut away.)

Failure of the screws holding them is the most common fault with any kind of handle. If the screw holes are enlarged plug them with filler or a piece of dowel, according to size. Use new screws when refitting the handles. Some handles are secured by a threaded metal rod with a nut on the end, and if this is missing replacement is not easy. An easier way is to put the rod into a little block of wood glued to the back of the drawer or door.

probably extend about 1cm ($\frac{1}{2}$in) into the wood (Fig 1). Scrape and file away any bits left behind. Cut the new rail to length: measure the distance between the legs, add the depth of both holes, then take off at least 6mm ($\frac{1}{4}$in) to give enough clearance to get it in (Fig 2).

Taper each end to fit into the holes; use one of the old stubs as a guide to draw a circle on the ends of the new rail. A spokeshave is the proper tool for shaping, otherwise use a trimming knife followed by a rasp or file. Finish off with abrasive paper. Test the rail in position: if it will not go in increase the depth of *one* of the holes; it should be a tight fit.

A rectangular rail is more difficult, but can be tackled provided it proves to have dowel joints and not mortise and tenons. The first step is to prepare a new rail complete with a dowel or dowels at one end. Glue this into the front leg. Prop the rail up into its correct position and drill right through the back leg and into the rail. Insert a dowel joint so that it sinks about 1cm ($\frac{1}{2}$in) into the leg and can be concealed with a wooden plug or filler.

REPLACING CASTORS

There are two basic kinds of castors on old furniture: cup castors, with a metal socket which fits over the leg; and screw castors which screw up inside the leg. If a castor is so badly worn that the wheel and/or the fork supporting it no longer moves freely it needs replacing.

To remove a cup castor (Fig 1) first undo the screw passing through its side, then pull it off, tapping the top with a hammer on a protective block of wood if necessary to free it. If the new castors are a little too tight chisel or rasp a bit off the wood; if too loose pack the space with slivers of card. Fill the old screw holes with plastic wood and drill pilot holes in the new positions.

On a screw castor (Fig 2) all the screws are on a plate underneath the leg; once these are undone, tap the plate sharply in an anticlockwise direction to free it and then unscrew. When fitting the new one put a small screwdriver blade into one screw hole and rest it against the shaft, so that you can turn the screw home instead of turning the castor mechanism. Some screw castors are fitted with a spiked plate (Fig 3) which just levers off.

Screw castors can split the bottoms of slender legs. Repair as for general splits, but afterwards it is safer to replace the castors with a cup type.

ADJUSTING HINGES

If a door will not shut or sags there is usually something wrong with its hinges. Unless perfectly adjusted no hinge will work properly. Both leaves must fit snugly into their recesses, being neither sunk into them, nor standing proud. It only takes a tiny obstruction, such as an insufficiently turned or over-size screw head, to prevent closure.

A common fault is that the weight of the door has pulled some of the screws loose, which is easily fixed provided you can get the old screws out. If the hinges look a bit worn it is a good idea to swap them top to bottom, as the top hinge takes most of the weight. Plug the holes and refit the hinges with new screws, if possible slightly longer than before.

If the door still does not close tightly, the fault may lie with the recesses. A too-deep recess may have been packed up with a thin piece of card, which has dropped out when screws worked loose. Alternatively, someone may have fitted new hinges that are slightly too thick so the recess needs chiselling out, but only a little. Close inspection and experiment should provide the answer.

When the hinges appear perfectly good the problem may be a warped or swollen door, which will need to have a little wood planed or rasped off where marks show that it is binding. However, do not rush to do this if a piece has come from a second hand shop or auction room. The cause may be damp, in which case if your home is properly heated and ventilated it will right itself.

If the screws once holding on a hinge have split the wood repair the split first according to the instructions for general splits.

REPAIRING DRAWERS

A sticking drawer can often be cured very simply by dusting the runners and rubbing them over with either a candle or a very soft drawing pencil. If you find deep grooves in the runners they need replacing. Unscrew or prise them off. Either use the same piece again, upside down, or obtain a new piece of hardwood. Another possibility is that one runner has dropped off – you may even find it in the drawer below. If the drawer wobbles about it means that guides fitted at the sides or centre are either missing or worn. Study a sound drawer to find out how both runners and guides are fitted and refit or replace them in the same way.

Common repairs needed to drawers :

runners loose

drawer sticking

central bearer loose

dovetail joints
out of alignment

Sometimes they are not glued, but held in what seems rather a casual way with a screw at one end; this is intentional to allow for differential movement in the timber carcass.

A drawer will also stick if it is damp, or out of shape. Let time cure damp, as for doors. If one or more of the dovetail joints at the corners is loose, vacuum out dust, squeeze in adhesive and tap it together, making sure the bottom is properly in place first. Check it for squareness, cramp up and leave to dry. If the whole drawer is dropping apart it will need to be taken to pieces and reassembled.

If a drawer sits too far back in its frame, spoiling the appearance of the chest, the reason is usually that small blocks of wood, the drawer stops, have gone missing. These should be placed somewhere on the drawer rails. Study another drawer, or look for telltale pale patches, to guide you in making a replacement. Glue the stop in place, then immediately slide the drawer in just far enough to push the block into the correct position. Secure it with a couple of fine panel pins.

A wide, deep drawer may stick fast because the thin bottom panel has sagged out of place. These are intentionally not glued, to allow for seasonal movement, but supported by a central bearer. This problem is easily cured by sliding the panel back into its grooves, then refixing the bearer.

REPAIRING DRAW LEAF TABLES

Problems with these can usually be solved by taking off the top and leaves and having a good look at their undersides. Check that screws holding the leaf bearers in place are all present and tight, or the leaves will sag when extended. If a bearer is badly warped it will bind, and needs replacing. There should also be stops underneath each bearer which prevent the leaves from being pulled out too far. The main table top should have a block screwed underneath which stops it moving sideways, and protective felt strips along each edge to prevent the leaves from being scratched.

REPAIRING DROP LEAF TABLES

The leaves on this type of table are supported by either an extra leg or by stays, and a good look at these will probably reveal the cause of any trouble. Stays may be wooden or metal, and the first thing to check is whether they are securely fixed. If broken or missing it may be possible to obtain a metal replacement for some types. Repairing them, or making new ones, calls for considerable skill. If the leaf droops because the stay is no longer holding it up at a right angle, fit a small wooden wedge to correct this.

On a gateleg table of the common sort, a weak point is the dowels which allow the gate to pivot out from the main table frame. If broken off or badly worn these can easily be repaired *if* the table is the type where the top dowel is in a recess cut in the side of the table frame and held in by a little block of wood. Unscrewing the block, if still present, enables the gate to be lifted out. Put new dowels into the gate post at top and bottom and screw on a new block or the existing one to secure the top dowel in place.

A gateleg table can be repaired by removing the block of wood and lifting out the gate.

REPAIRING UNEVEN LEGS

Find out which leg is short by standing a chair on a level table top; move a large table around to alter the leg positions. Put packing under the short leg to find out how much adjustment is needed. If it is very little a piece of packing material glued on will not be noticeable. On a large leg use hardboard or plywood (remove layers of ply to get the thickness required). On a small chair leg it is easier to cut a piece of carpet or rubber; anything durable will do. If the gap is quite large, or you are a perfectionist, use the packing as a measure for removing the required amount from the other three legs.

WOODWORKING ADHESIVES

Old furniture is normally glued together with animal glue, often called Scotch glue. You can tell it by its pale brown appearance; when very old it separates into crystals. As it is inferior to modern woodworking adhesives, and has to be used hot, there is no reason why you should bother with it for repairing ordinary furniture. A professional restorer would use it on antiques, but today's craftsmen in wood, making new furniture, use modern PVA woodworking adhesive, and so should you. The only thing to bear in mind is that you must remove every trace of old animal glue first; this is not difficult as any that does not scrape off can be steamed off.

PVA (polyvinyl acetate) This is sold under a number of different brand names, but is always a creamy white, and usually labelled woodworking adhesive. It is applied to one surface of the wood liberally; any that squeezes out should be wiped off immediately with a damp cloth. The joins thus made need to be lightly cramped or weighted for at least 30 minutes while the adhesive sets. Leaving it overnight does no harm, as the bond will not reach full strength for 24 hours. PVA is clean and easy to use, extremely strong and suitable for all general woodwork except outdoor furniture, as being water-based it gradually breaks down if exposed to rain and damp conditions.

Contact adhesives As weighting a joint may be impossible, and cramping very awkward, you may wonder why you cannot use one of these, which make a bond almost immediately. The main reason is that joins made in wood with contact adhesive are almost impossible to get apart. This can be a serious drawback, if say you realise too late that a part is on back to front, or you have used the wrong one. Nevertheless, it does have a place, mainly for gluing back missing pieces of moulding or anything else quite impossible to cramp. But make sure you get the position right first time! Contact adhesives are usually sold for fixing plastic laminate to worktops, and are often thixotropic – jelly-like. They used to bond instantly, but the latest versions give a few minutes in which to slide the pieces into the correct position. The adhesive is applied to both surfaces of the wood and left to become almost dry before they are put together.

Contact adhesive is also used for gluing large sheets of veneer. Small pieces, such as loose marquetry work, can be also fixed with PVA.

Urea formaldehyde This is a type of woodworking adhesive with greater moisture resistance than PVA, and which also has gap-filling properties. Therefore, it can be useful to mend a badly-fitting joint, or for outdoor furniture.

Glue film This is a new invention specially designed for laying sheets of veneer; it is clean and easy to use, and ensures that the right amount of adhesive is automatically spread all over the groundwork. It is available, together with instructions for use, from veneer suppliers.

Other adhesives The very strong adhesives – epoxy resins used for china repairs, and the new super-glues – are expensive, and not necessary for joining wood. But if you have some and only want to make a small repair there is no reason not to use it.

CHEMICAL STRIPPERS

There are two basic types: the well-established liquid ones, and the new peel-off pastes. Both are powerful substances, but quite safe provided you follow the instructions carefully: wear gloves and immediately wash off any chemicals that splash on you. If possible work outdoors or in a garage; otherwise stand the piece in the centre of the room, well away from anything else, and protect the floor covering with thick layers of newspaper, ideally topped with a sheet of polythene. Both types are spread on and left for a specified time, when the dissolved finish is scraped or peeled off, and the piece rinsed clean, usually with water.

Liquid stripper is cheaper, but it only removes one or two layers of paint or varnish at a time, so several applications are frequently needed. It works quickly, in about 15 minutes, but must be removed by scraping, which carries the risk of damaging the wood, which also gets softened by its application.

The big advantage of the peel-off type is that once they have penetrated all the layers – and they can act on ten or more – they are simply peeled away; no scraping is necessary. However, this takes time – up to 15 hours – during which the stripper has to be kept moist. Peel-off stripper also works out rather expensive, as it has to be applied very thickly, but for stripping pieces with elaborately turned legs, mouldings and carving it is more satisfactory. Used on pine it has a slight yellowing effect which is not unattractive. It is very important not to miss the tiniest spot anywhere, or this will be forever whiter.

Peel-off stripper is for wood only; liquid stripper can also be used on metal fittings, which it does very well.

Commercial stripping firms dip furniture in tanks of hot caustic soda. This is extremely efficient, but takes all the natural oils out of the wood, turning it greyish and sometimes causing cracking and a constant recurrence of white crystals on the surface. (Veneered pieces and bentwood chairs should never be dipped as they will come apart in the tank.) Although you can buy caustic soda, you can only use it cold, and it is not really advisable as it is so highly corrosive. It must be washed away afterwards with gallons of water, so it is not really a practical proposition unless you happen to have a large area to work in, with a central drain. If you do use it wear heavy-duty rubber gloves, wellingtons and old clothes covering arms and legs.

SANDING AND SCRAPING

Sanding can be done by hand or machine, but the former is much too gentle for anything but finishing off. Machine sanding is particularly effective when deep blemishes such as burns have scarred the wood, as it removes a thin layer, exposing clean new wood below. All sanding (and scraping) should be carried out in the direction of the grain, or ineradicable scratches will appear; this is not possible with some powered sanding equipment.

The basic technique, by hand or machine, is to start with coarse abrasive paper and progress through medium to fine so that you end up with a really smooth surface. Never rub over corners or edges or they will lose their shape. The better-quality (silicon carbide) paper is preferable to ordinary glass paper for use on furniture, and the new self-adhesive types speed up fitting the paper to whatever tool is being used.

To hand sand flat areas use the abrasive paper wrapped round a cork block. On turned legs, rails or dowels use small strips folded in half; on fancy mouldings or carving use fine steel wool (grade oo). Patent hand-sanding tools are also useful. These are basically just plastic handles with variously shaped sanding heads taking stick-on abrasive paper. There are small narrow ones for reaching awkward spots, large flat ones, and one with an adjustable head designed for gently curved surfaces.

Scraping is usually used in conjunction with chemical stripping, but can be effective on its own, if the old finish is very brittle and flaky. Hardwoods are supposed to be scraped and not sanded as scraping does not produce grain-clogging dust. The traditional craftsman's cabinet scraper takes skill both to use and to keep sharp. A better tool for the amateur is a patent scraper with a handle; these are available in a variety of shapes and sizes, and the blades are replaceable.

Decorators' scrapers, called shave hooks, can be used, but only if new and razor-sharp. There are two kinds, the triangular shave hook for flat surfaces, and the combination shave hook which tackles curves as well. For gentle scraping to remove liquid chemical stripper and old paint use a stripping knife.

If you have a power tool various attachments can be used with it for power sanding. The basic rubber pad, used with a disc of abrasive paper on top, is a very coarse method which leaves circular marks on the wood. It is, therefore, only suitable for removing upper layers of paint, or for a complete job if the piece is to be repainted. An orbital sander (this can be an attachment or a separate tool) also leaves circles on the wood, but these are very tiny, do not go deep and so can be removed with a final hand sanding. Also known as a finishing sander, this has a far gentler action than a disc. Both these can only be used on flat surfaces.

For gentle curves, like the seat of a kitchen chair, or a back rest, a drum sanding attachment is useful. This is more vigorous than the orbital sander, but gentler than a disc. It can be used on flat surfaces too, but with caution – keep it constantly sweeping over the surface or hollows will develop. An alternative is an abrasive flap wheel, which can be used on any surface. Being small, this is ideal for getting into tight spots. The tool consists of lots of little flaps of abrasive paper mounted to form a small wheel. Their action is gentler than that of the drum sander. Both these attachments, correctly used, rotate in the direction of the grain, so leave no marks behind.

Only the disc sander, or a drum fitted with very coarse paper, are quick methods of removing layers of paint. The other two *can* be used – and may have to be when surfaces are not flat – but progress is slow. They are best for finishing off after using liquid stripper, to remove any residue of the old finish and get the wood really clean and smooth.

FILLING AND SMOOTHING

Before proceeding to staining and/or finishing fill any holes and cracks as described on page 11.

In the old days craftsmen would fill the grain of open-pored hardwoods with grain filler before applying French polish. This speeds the way to a mirror-like gloss by preventing the first coats from sinking into the wood. You may see traces of grain filler if you have stripped the piece, in the form of pale flecks in the grain. Although grain filling is by no means essential, it is a good idea *if* the original filler has been removed by machine sanding, and *if* you want a very high gloss. Proprietary grain filler is a thick paste, supplied in various colours to match different woods. To apply simply thin it to a creamy consistency with white spirit and rub it hard *across* the grain of the wood with a coarse rag. Once all the pores have been filled rub off the surplus filler quickly before it sets.

The final job is to make sure that all parts of the item are sanded perfectly smooth, and brush off every speck of dust. Allow time for dust in the air to settle before applying any kind of new finish.

STAINING

If after stripping the piece has a bleached look, or still bears traces of old stain, tinting it with wood stain is the answer. Staining can also make anaemic-looking whitewood furniture look far more interesting, but remember that wood in a bare state does not show the colour that will be obtained after applying a clear finish. To get a fairly good idea of what this will be dab the wood with water or white spirit; while wet the colour will approximate to that obtained after finishing.

Wood stains are available in a wide range of timber shades, from pale pine to black oak; colours can be mixed together if required, but keep to the same brand. Only one coat is necessary, and the secret of success is to get this on evenly, without overlaps. You can use a brush or a pad of cloth; a large paint pad is excellent for big items like a table top. Whichever you use, work in the direction of the grain only – do not use the criss-cross action employed to brush out paint. Some stains are water based, and raise the grain slightly when applied; their instructions will recommend that before starting you should wet the surfaces with water, allow to dry and sand smooth. Others are spirit based and can be applied straight away.

Shade guides for wood stains show the colour achieved on neutral coloured wood *after varnishing*. This colour can be seen during application, while the stain is wet, but fades as the stain dries. The true colour emerges after finishing; but it may be slightly different from that shown on the shade guide because of the original colour of your wood. So if trying to match in a repair made with new wood, always test the stain underneath, and assess it while wet.

An alternative to staining and then putting varnish or another clear finish on top is to use a tinted polyurethane varnish. These behave differently from stains in that the colour deepens with each coat: shade cards show the full colour obtained after a number of coats on pale wood, and your first coat or two will look very wishy-washy. Tinted varnishes are available in a number of wood tones, rather fewer than for wood stains. It is also possible to get polyurethane varnish tinted with bright colours such as red, yellow or green, but these are not so widely stocked.

FINISHING

Although clear polyurethane varnish is today's most popular finish, it is by no means the only thing available. Cold cure lacquer, French polish, paint and oil all have their place. Which one you choose is partly a matter of personal taste, but should also be appropriate to the furniture involved, and the use it is going to get.

Whatever the finish, never forget that dust is enemy No. 1. Do not work in a dirty, dusty environment; have the piece in a room where you can shut the door and leave it undisturbed while the finish dries. Immediately before applying any finish go over the wood with a rag just dampened with white spirit to remove any tiny specks of dust; also finger marks which are always slightly oily. Do the same before each new coat, particularly if any sanding has been done.

Polyurethane varnish One of the great modern inventions, this is easily applied by brush, and stands up to any amount of heat, spills and hard knocks. Most brands nowadays are used straight from the tin. Polyurethane varnish can give a glossy, satin or matt finish; it is usually clear, but can also be tinted. One characteristic of polyurethane varnish that may not always be desirable is that it darkens with age. This can sometimes be a positive advantage, as it causes pine or whitewood, which is very pale initially, to take on a richer golden glow with every passing year.

FRENCH POLISHING FOR BEGINNERS

French polish comes under several different names. The basic ones available in small quantities for the amateur restorer are French polish, which gives a rich brown colour, and is suitable for mahogany and similar woods; button polish, which gives a slightly harder and more orange finish; and white polish, which is bleached and meant for pale woods. If working on bare wood you will need quite a lot of polish; the smallest-sized bottles are only enough for refinishing work or something very small. In addition to the polish you will need small bottles of linseed oil and methylated spirit; a piece of cotton the size of a man's handkerchief; some cotton wool; fine (flour grade) abrasive paper; a large screw-topped jar and some rag. The cloth and cotton wool are used to make the rubber, the traditional applicator pad. The type of cloth is important, as a weak, fibre-shedding material will break down under the prolonged rubbing and shed bits all over the work.

As when varnishing you must work in a dust-free atmosphere. It must also be warm and dry, as cold and damp make the finish go cloudy. Put the item near a window so you have a good light to help spot any blemishes.

If the piece is being refinished simply clean it as described on page 8. If it has been stripped it should be sanded absolutely smooth. Ensure there is no dust anywhere. Prepare the rubber: place a handful of cotton wool in the centre of the cloth (Fig 1), hold it in the palm of your hand and pour on just enough polish to saturate the cotton wool without dripping (Fig 2). Gather up the ends of the cloth and twist them around. If too much polish appears on the face of the pad blot it on a scrap of wood. Lubricate the pad with the merest drop of linseed oil – just what you get on a fingertip held over the neck of the bottle.

Spread the polish evenly and sparingly over the surface, using circular or figure of eight movements (Fig 3). The trick is never to let the rubber stop on the surface – keep sweeping it on and off the edges. As the polish gets used up the rubber will start to drag. It is better to force out more polish by squeezing it harder than relubricating it with oil, as too much oil causes a smeary finish. If the furniture has internal corners work the rubber into a point to get into them. On complicated mouldings and carving apply the polish sparingly with a small soft paint brush. Take great

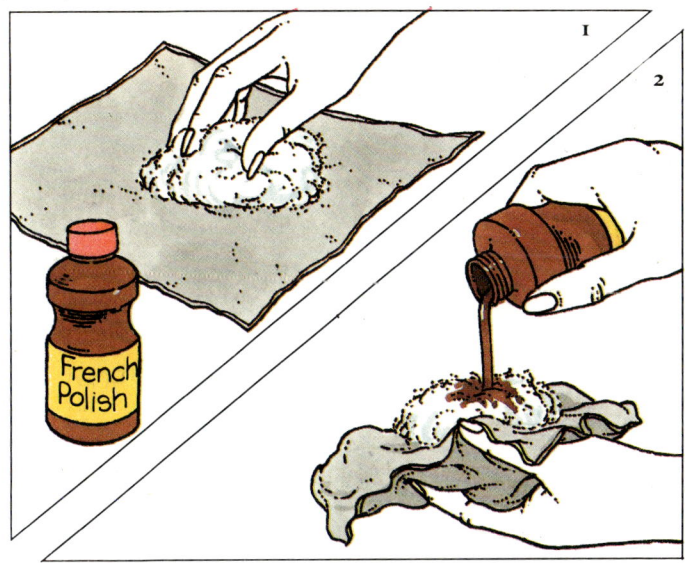

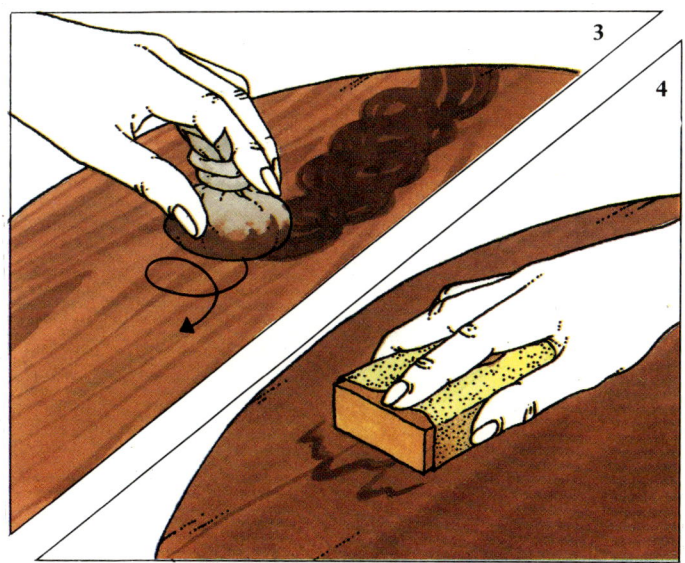

care always to wipe off the tiniest run or pool of polish before it sets. Put the rubber in the screwtop jar to keep it moist, go away and leave the polish to dry. About 20 minutes should be enough, but longer does no harm.

The first coat may raise the grain of the wood. If so rub the surface very lightly with flour-grade abrasive paper (Fig 4 previous page) and wipe off the dust with a rag. Continue to build up coats, pouring more polish into the rubber and relubricating it if necessary, until you achieve the finish you want. Before applying each new coat inspect the work carefully for blemishes such as rubber marks, runs or dust specks and if present rub them lightly away. After five coats leave the work overnight to harden before going any further. If you are refinishing a piece, one or two coats may be quite adequate. On bare wood ten coats may be sufficient if you do not want a particularly high gloss; but an old-fashioned mirror finish may take 20 or more.

However many coats, the last one gets special treatment to arrive at the perfect finish. Have the rubber almost dry of polish and thin what there is by pouring a few drops of methylated spirit on to the face. Then rub the work over with long strokes back and forth along the direction of the grain (Fig 5). As soon as the rubber drags add a little more methylated spirit. Leave the job for about a week to give the polish time to harden before anything touches it.

5 *Apply the final coat of French polish and allow it time to harden.*

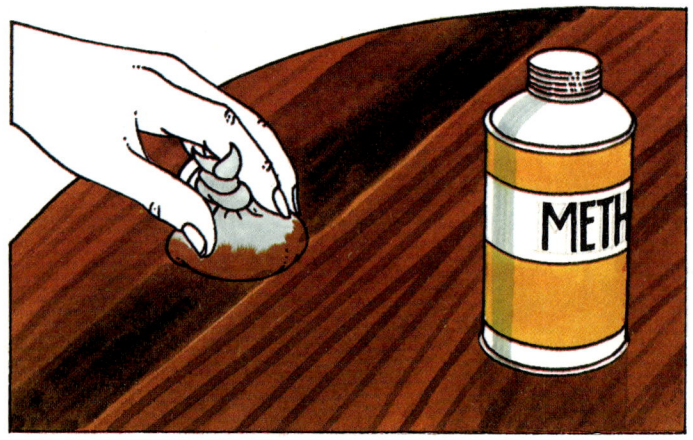

French polishing kit French polishing can also be done with a kit consisting of two bottles. One contains slightly thinned polish which requires no lubricating; the second is a finishing liquid. This is slightly abrasive and can also be used to remove minor blemishes, so the kit is particularly good for use on existing French polish or cellulose varnish. Instructions for use are included.

Cold cure lacquer Also known as hardset or plastic coating, this is even more hardwearing than polyurethane, and is frequently used on bar counters. It is supplied in two parts, lacquer and hardener, which are mixed together and applied by brush, then burnished to a high gloss when dry. (A satin or matt finish can be obtained by rubbing the surface over with fine steel wool instead, followed by wax polish.) Cold cure lacquer is not as popular as polyurethane varnish, as it is more expensive, and more trouble to use. Also brushes have to be cleaned in special solvent. However, it has two other great virtues: it dries in only one hour, and can be recoated in two; and it retains its clarity with age. If you are hesitating as to whether to go to the trouble of French polishing a dining table, knowing that it is bound to get marked, cold cure lacquer is the answer.

Paint This is the finish for hiding a poor-quality or dull-looking wood, and for giving solid colour. The major brands are now all of the easy-brush clean type, which means that brushes can be washed out in detergent and hot water, thus greatly reducing the chore of cleaning up afterwards. The range of colours is enormous, and most standard paints are available in either gloss or satin finish. The former is more durable and covers better.

Painting furniture must be done with a great deal more care than painting structural woodwork, or the end result will look cheap and nasty. Also bear in mind that no paint will stand up to abrasion, so it is not a good finish for table tops and the like. In such cases either protect the top with a cloth or glass; or use a different material such as plastic laminate.

It is not necessary to strip a piece of furniture to get a good paint finish, but the surface *must* be flat; any lumps, pimples or chips in the old finish will be faithfully reproduced in the new. It must also be sound – anything that is flaking off will continue to do so, taking the new paint with it. Even if the old paint or varnish is in good condition it must be thoroughly sanded, or the new paint will adhere feebly to the glossy surface and chip off at the slightest knock. (An alternative is to wipe on liquid sander, a new product which cleans and keys paint in one go.) The surface must also be completely free of any dirt, oil, wax, grease etc. (see cleaning, page 8).

If the piece has been stripped start with a coat of primer. Otherwise, or next, use an undercoat, which forms a slightly rough base coat for the top coat of gloss. Follow the manufacturer's instructions regarding any rubbing down between coats, drying time and recommended number of top coats. Brush the paint well out with a criss-cross action to ensure that you do not get any disfiguring runs, particularly on ledges. Keep an eagle eye open for any foreign bodies such as flies or hairs and lift them off with a clean artist's paint brush. Give the paint plenty of time not only to dry, but reach its full hardness, before using the furniture.

Oil Although this is a finish with limited uses today it still has its place, if you want a quick job that calls for no skill whatsoever, and do not require high gloss or hardwearing properties. The trouble with linseed oil is that it takes so long to dry; even boiled linseed oil, which has driers added, still takes up to 24 hours. A high gloss can be obtained, but only with great labour, applying 'once a day for a week, once a week for a month and once a month for a year'. Modern teak oil is much better: it is simply wiped on with a soft cloth (two or three coats are sufficient) and the drying time is only 4–6 hours. This finish does not give a protective surface to the wood, but seals it, enriches the colour and stops it getting dirty.

WOODWORM

A scattering of small, round holes and tiny piles of fine sawdust repeatedly appearing on the floor underneath old wooden furniture, shows the telltale signs that it has played host to the larvae of the common furniture beetle. You may also spot an adult beetle in the late spring – they are small dark brown chunky creatures, about 4mm ($\frac{3}{16}$in) long, with rows of tiny holes decorating their wing cases. Even if there are only a few holes treatment is essential as there is no certain way of telling whether the worm is still present.

The holes are *not* entrance holes; they only show where the adult beetle bit its way out and flew away. When the beetle emerges it is quite likely to lay its eggs on the same piece of furniture, and the grubs, or woodworm, spend the next *three years* tunnelling inside and eating the wood, before they pupate and emerge as a new generation of beetles.

Treatment for woodworm is quite simple: you need a small quantity of proprietary woodworm killer and an injector bottle. Use the injector to get the fluid flowing through the tunnels; they interconnect, so you only need to treat them at about 5cm (2in) intervals if they are numerous. Then brush the fluid over every surface, making sure you do not miss the unpolished wood on the back, inside and underneath, and not forgetting the feet. As the fluid is slightly oily leave the piece for a week or two to dry out.

If a piece seems untouched a good precaution is to use an insecticidal polish but put the first application on all surfaces, not just the polished ones.

REPAIRING CANE, WICKER AND BAMBOO FURNITURE

Wicker items are not easily repaired, beyond binding up loose fastenings. A wicker, or rattan, chair with a sagging bottom can be kept in use by fixing a board underneath and hiding the damage with a cushion. Bamboo furniture is mainly nailed together and proper repairs are difficult as the old nails split the bamboo. However, it displays a remarkable ability to hold together if helped along with a few new nails, in different places if possible.

Table tops can be greatly improved by replacing the covering – often nasty-looking plastic has been put on; the proper material is grass cloth. Cane and wicker work materials should be obtainable from a local craft shop; small pieces of bamboo can be cut from garden canes if required.

CANING—
MATERIALS AND TOOLS REQUIRED

Cane Cane for chair seats comes from South-East Asia and is available in two qualities, blue tie and red tie. Blue tie is the best one to use as the quality of the cane is better, so less is discarded from the bundle as you work your seat. Cane is graded in sizes 1 to 6, the smaller the size the thinner the cane. The two sizes most commonly used for caning chairs are No. 2 and No. 4, with No. 6 and No. 2 used for the optional beading edge. The cane size depends on the distance between the holes on the chair seat; 13mm ($\frac{1}{2}$in) is the usual distance between holes, but if the holes are closer together use two finer canes to prevent over-crowding. You can always check the size with the cane you are replacing, if you can depend upon the previous weaver. Also, if you are only caning one chair it is more economical to use only one size cane, No. 4; cane is sold in bundles and working with two sizes will mean left-over material, as one bundle is more than

sufficient for one chair. As to the cost, the thicker the cane size the cheaper the bundle.

Pegs Pegs can be divided into temporary or permanent pegs. Temporary pegs are used to hold the cane in place during weaving and these are cut from thick centre cane. However, golf tees make a good substitute. When finishing the seat, pegs can be used to hold the cane permanently in place, and for this purpose a medium-sized centre cane or pared down matchsticks (with their heads removed) are the best answer.

Scissors and sharp knife These two are used to remove the old cane from the chair; to cut the new cane and if necessary to sharpen the cane end into a point to help with the weaving.

Clearer This is a small pointed tool used to clear the holes of old cane. A good alternative is a long nail or a fine metal knitting needle. Check the thickness of the tool with the hole size and do not force it down the holes as it will disfigure the chair.

Small hammer A hammer taps the permanent pegs into the holes and flattens any finishing knots at the end of the work.

REMOVING THE OLD CANE

Before re-caning, all the old cane must be stripped from the chair and the chair frame repaired and finished, as this cannot be done after re-caning.

First, cut away the cane close to the chair frame, then knock out any old pegs and clear each hole in turn. If the seat has been woven in a complicated pattern, or the seat is shaped, it is a good idea to use the old cane as a rough guide when working the new seat, so keep it until you have finished.

PREPARING THE CANE

Dry cane is quicker to pull through the work, but the cane will be easier on the hands if it is dipped into hot water. Do not soak the cane, but pass it through a bowl of water as you work, running your fingers along the underside of the cane. Only prepare the cane you need and do not leave any wrapped up in a damp fabric. Before you begin, discard any split, damaged or discoloured cane, as this will spoil the appearance and durability of the chair.

TRADITIONAL SEVEN-STEP PATTERN

This pattern is the one most commonly used to re-cane a chair seat or back, when working on a square or rectangular chair. It can also be successfully adapted to suit a shaped or round seat.

Step 1: the first setting Using the thinner of the two canes, No. 2 (if two sizes are to be used) place the first length in the hole next to the back left-hand corner hole on the back rail of the chair with the glossy side uppermost. Leave about 15cm ($\frac{5}{8}$in) hanging down below the base of the hole and temporarily peg in place. Carry the length of cane vertically across the seat base and into the exact opposite hole, still keeping the cane with the glossy side uppermost and making sure that the cane is not twisted. Keeping the cane fairly taut, temporarily peg into this hole. Bring the

cane up through the next hole in the front rail, untwisted, with the glossy side uppermost. This side should always be uppermost, even on the underside of the seat base. Peg the cane in place again. Take the cane to the back of the seat and through the opposite hole on the back rail and peg in place again. Once the cane has passed on, the temporary pegs can be removed and replaced in the next hole, but leave the first peg in place as it holds the cane end. Continue, working backwards and forwards in this way, keeping the cane tension fairly tight and even. Each setting and weaving will tighten the seat, so do not pull the cane too tight with this first setting, but on the other hand do not let the work sag. If the cane runs out, leave the end protruding from the underneath of the rail and peg the last hole to secure it until the seat is finished and the ends can be woven in. The cane can never end in the middle of the seat. Start the new length of cane in the next hole in the sequence in the same way as before, pegging it in place to hold.

Step 2: the first weaving This is worked in exactly the same way as step 1, but over the canes of step 1 at right angles, treating the side rails as the back and front rails.

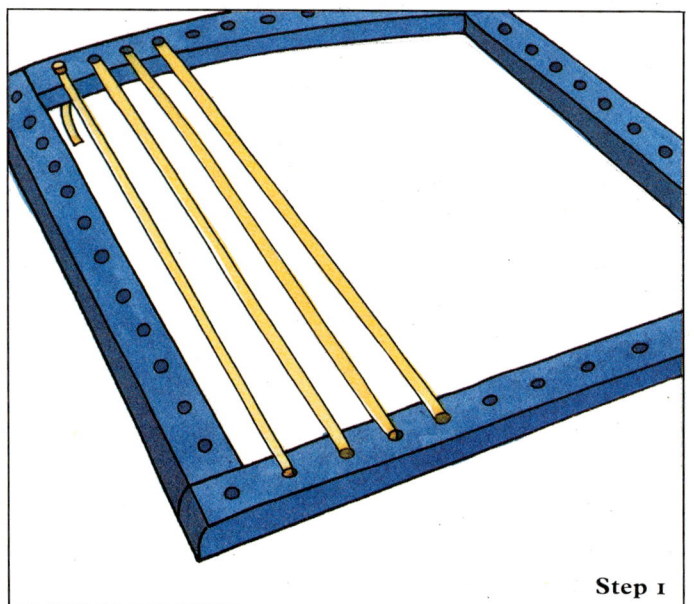

Step 1

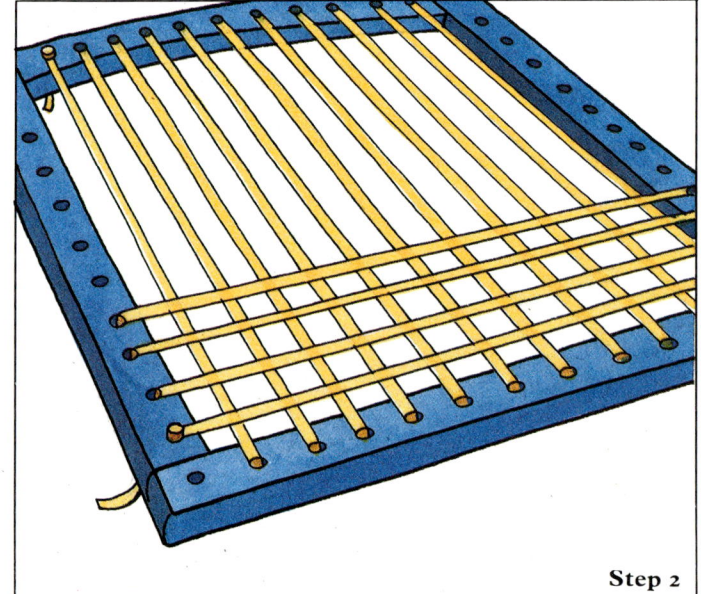

Step 2

Step 3: the second setting Step 3 is the repeat of step 1 again on top of the previous two steps, creating a sandwich of vertical strands with a horizontal centre strand. As you work, position the cane from this step parallel and to the right of the previous vertical step. Remember to keep the cane with the glossy side uppermost, as there will be no room to correct it once the cane has been pulled through the hole, except by unpicking the work. When you reach a hole that has been temporarily pegged, remove the peg, insert the working cane and repeg the hole, keeping the end tightly in place.

Step 4: the second weaving This step follows the same pattern as the first horizontal step, step 2, but the cane is woven over and under the vertical strands. Still keeping the cane glossy side up, weave the working cane through about 6 to 8 vertical pairs before pulling the cane completely through, as it makes for a more even and tighter fabric. Do not worry if the cane lines look uneven, as the following diagonal steps will pull them into place. To begin, thread the cane end underneath the cane of the first setting, up between the two vertical canes and over the second setting.

Repeat with each pair of canes. Continue working from side to side, joining in new canes as required and pegging protruding ends. Remember to always work each row in the same way, under the first setting and over the second setting. Try to keep the pattern correct, as the only way to alter it once it has been woven, is to unpick the work.

Step 5: the first diagonal If you are working with two different size canes, now is the time to change to the thicker cane, No. 4. Peg the cane end into the back left-hand corner hole. Begin weaving over the first pair, the horizontals, moving over to the right by going under the vertical pair then over the next horizontal pair. The weaving will seem to be done in steps, but once the cane is pulled through it forms a diagonal line. Where the seat is completely square you will end the first row in the opposite corner, otherwise thread the cane into whichever hole is naturally reached. Bring the cane up through the next hole to the left on the front rail and weave back to the top in the same way. Continue, until the first corner is reached, and then weave the second half of the seat in the same way. In the diagonal rows the corner holes are used twice.

Step 3

Step 4

Step 5

Step 6: the second diagonal Step 6 is the exact opposite to step 5; this time the cane is woven under the horizontals and over the verticals, making up the finished square pattern.

Step 6

Tying in To finish off each loose cane end that protrudes beneath the seat base, tie the end round an adjacent loop. Wet the cane end first to remove any brittleness. Cut each end into a point. Push the end under the adjacent loop twice and pull tight. Tap the coil gently with a hammer and cut off the end. On chair backs it is best to permanently peg in the cane ends as tying in the cane will look unsightly.

Step 7: beading This is the modern way to finish off the edge of the caning and never used on antique chairs. A thick cane is couched with a length of thin cane round the outer edge of the seat to cover the holes. If this method is not used, permanently peg each hole instead. Hammer the permanent pegs into the holes, making sure of a tight fit and clip off flush with the chair seat on the top and underneath. Another alternative finish is to peg alternate holes and couch the beading into the unpegged holes. For the beading, use a size 6 cane, couching it down with a No. 2 cane; here again, finer canes can be used if necessary. Begin by inserting a length of No. 2 cane into the hole next to a corner. Allow this end to protrude 4cm (1½in) above the top. Bend this end into the next hole and bring the working end up through the same hole, thus securing the end in place. Insert a length of No. 6 cane – long enough to complete the side being worked in one piece – into the same hole and lay it along the row of holes. Pass the thinner cane over the thicker cane and take it down into the same hole. Pass the thin cane up the next hole from the underside, remembering to keep it untwisted and with the glossy side uppermost. Continue to the opposite corner hole and then insert both canes into this hole. Begin again for the adjacent side, pegging all the ends firmly into the corner hole. Repeat to finish off each side in turn.

Step 7

SHAPED SEATS

If the seat is wider at the front than the back, begin the caning in the centre of the chair instead of at one side. When you reach the back corners you will find you still have empty holes on the front rail. Continue working into these holes taking the cane into holes on the side rails. These extra side canes are called short strokes. On the diagonal steps not only will the corner holes be used twice but also some holes on the side edges; these will not be noticed once the chair seat is complete. Work in the same way on circular seats.

UPHOLSTERY

Upholstery transforms a flat, uncomfortable chair into a treasured piece of furniture that has a long and useful life. One of the rules of upholstery is to use the same materials that were originally used on the chair.

MATERIALS AND TOOLS REQUIRED

Mallet and ripping chisel Used for lifting the heads of tacks when removing old upholstery. The chisel has a blunt head to prevent it from damaging the wood.

Tack lifter For the same use as above. As an alternative, use a pair of pliers.

Hammer Use a small-headed hammer.

Web strainer/stretcher This is used for stretching the webbing across the seat of the chair. Alternatively you can use a block of wood and wrap the webbing firmly round it to pull the webbing taut.

Needles A 20–25cm (8–10in) upholsterers' needle, which has points at both ends. Half-circular needles are used to stitch on the springs.

Webbing The best webbing to use is the 5cm (2in) wide black and white flax webbing with a twill weave. This is important as it forms the basis of all the upholstery.

Springs Use 10cm (4in) coil springs made in 12mm (gauge 10) wire.

Tacks These are used to attach the various materials to the chair frame. Use 13mm ($\frac{1}{2}$in) fine tacks for hessian, scrim and top covers and 15mm ($\frac{5}{8}$in) improved tacks for the webbing and laid cord. Improved tacks have larger heads and fatter bodies than fine tacks.

Hessian For covering the webbing to prevent the filling from falling out.

Filling Horsehair is expensive and not readily available, but a mixture of horse and animal hair is available, the longer and curlier the better. Re-use the horsehair type filling from the stripped chair, if possible, adding extra if necessary. To wash animal hair pull the old hair apart in a sink full of tepid water.

Pull out and discard old twine, tacks, etc. Rinse well in clean water and spin dry wrapped in an old pillowcase. Spread out on newspaper to dry thoroughly before re-use.

Twine This is a very strong, smooth string made from flax and hemp and used for bridle ties and for stitching the springs in place.

Laid cord A thicker twine used for lacing the springs.

Scrim A loosely woven hessian-type fabric which is used for covering the first layer of filling.

Calico A strong, closely-woven unbleached fabric used to cover the second layer of filling under the top cover.

Wadding A thick cotton-based fabric which comes in different weights (thicknesses) which is used over the filling to prevent the filling from working its way out of the chair.

Main fabric Choose a proper upholstery weight of fabric which will wear well.

Braid Choose a similar width braid to the original and as close in colour to the main fabric as possible. Use with clear fabric adhesive.

Bottoming Black linen fabric applied to the underside of the chair to finish it off. Alternatively use hessian.

STRIPPING OFF THE OLD UPHOLSTERY

Work over old newspaper to catch the old materials and the dust! Use the ripping chisel and mallet to remove the old tacks, always working with the grain of the wood. Cut through any twine and ties with scissors. Repair and treat the chair frame as necessary.

DROP-IN SEAT

Webbing Remove the seat from the chair. Use 15mm ($\frac{5}{8}$in) improved tacks to hold the webbing in place. The strands of the webbing should be evenly spaced across the seat and the spaces between each length of webbing should never be wider than the width of the webbing. Try to avoid the old tack holes by placing the new webbing slightly to one side of the old webbing positions. On small drop-in seats there should be at least two strands of webbing across the seat in both directions; use three strands on larger seats. If the seat front is larger than the seat back, slightly splay out the webbing on either side of the central strand when fixing to the front rail. Attach the webbing to the top of the frame, unless there are springs to accommodate, in which case attach the webbing to the underside of the frame. Working from the roll of webbing to avoid waste, turn under 2.5cm (1in) and place it about 13mm ($\frac{1}{2}$in) in from the edge of the back frame. Secure in place with five 15mm ($\frac{5}{8}$in) improved tacks – place one tack through the fold at each corner and one in the centre. Place the remaining two tacks on the inside edge in between the three previous tacks, forming a W shape. Either using a webbing strainer/stretcher or piece of wood, tighten the webbing until it is taut over the front rail. Hold it in place with three tacks in a row, placed through the single thickness of webbing. Cut off the excess webbing, leaving 2.5cm (1in) overlap. Turn the

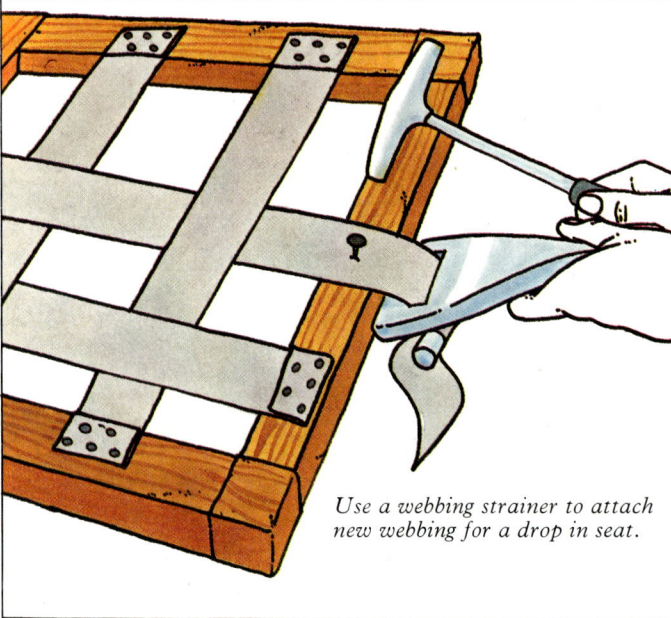

Use a webbing strainer to attach new webbing for a drop in seat.

overlap back on itself and place two more tacks through the double webbing a line nearer to the centre of the seat and in between the three previous tacks to form a W shape. Repeat for the remaining strands of webbing, completing the webbing in one direction before webbing in the opposite direction. When webbing in the opposite direction, interweave the webbing before tacking in position.

Hessian Measure across the seat at its widest part and add 5cm (2in) to the measurement for turnings. Measure from back to front of the seat and add an allowance as before. Cut out a piece of hessian on the straight of grain to these measurements. Place the hessian centrally over the webbing. Fold up 2.5cm (2in) allowance all round the seat. Tack in place through the folded hessian edge with 13mm ($\frac{1}{2}$in) fine tacks placed about 4cm ($1\frac{1}{2}$in) apart, keeping the fabric grain straight and stretching the hessian taut as you tack.

Stretch the hessian taut and tack it round the edges of the seat.

Bridle ties These are twine loops which are made in the hessian to hold the filling in place. Thread a length of twine on to a half-circular needle, long enough to go twice round the seat. Secure with a slip knot at the right-hand front corner, 7.5cm (3in) from both front and side edges. Work round the seat making a series of 2.5cm (1in) long back stitches and leaving loops in between large enough to slide a flattened hand underneath.

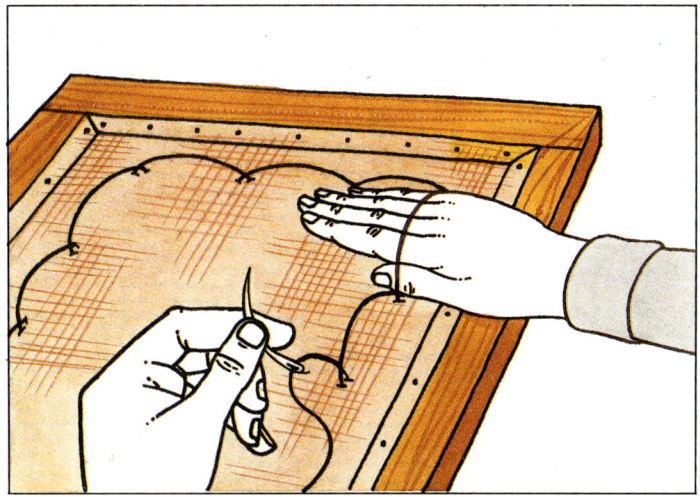

Filling Tease out any lumps in the hair filling. Place small portions of the filling under the bridle ties, working from the middle of the seat outwards. As you work, keep the filling even and tightly packed, using enough to give the seat a rounded shape. Remember that with use hair filling will pack down, so make sure that it is tightly packed in place.

Wadding Measure from the outside top edge of the side frame over the filling to the other side at the widest part of the seat. Measure from back to front in the same way. Cut out one piece of wadding to these measurements. Place the wadding centrally over the filling.

Calico Measure from the bottom of the seat rail on one side over the top of the seat to the opposite side rail, again over the widest part of the seat. Measure from back to front in the same way. Cut out a piece of calico to these measurements, following the straight of grain. Lay the calico centrally over the wadding on the seat. Temporarily tack the calico to the underside of the back of the frame using 13mm ($\frac{1}{2}$in) fine tacks

about 1cm ($\frac{3}{8}$in) from the edge and spaced about 2.5cm (1in) apart, leaving the calico free 5cm (2in) from both corners. Stand the frame on the back edge and pull the calico forward over the front rail. The calico must be pulled as tight as possible. Hammer in a temporary tack to attach the calico to the underside of the seat frame. Pull the calico forward in this way for every temporary tack. Work outwards from the centre, placing the tacks as for the seat back to within 5cm (2in) of the corners. Keep checking that the wadding has not moved from its central position over the filling. Attach the calico centrally to the underside of the seat on each side with a temporary tack. Pull the calico from the middle of the sides outwards and temporary tack both sides to within 5cm (2in) of the corners. At each corner, pull the calico over the corner and fix in place with a temporary tack. Fold in the excess fabric to form pleats facing towards the corner; trim away excess fabric from inside the fabric fold and temporarily tack in place. Check the shape of the seat and run your hand across the seat to check for any lumps. When you are satisfied with the finish, hammer home all the tacks.

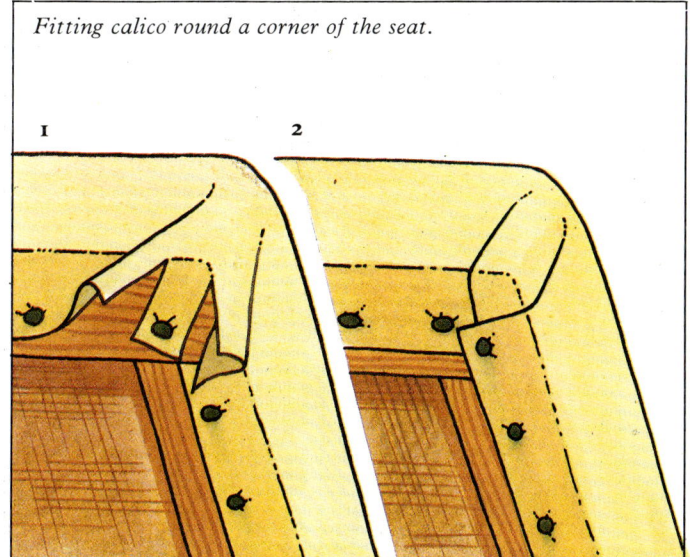

Fitting calico round a corner of the seat.

Main cover fabric The top cover is placed on the seat and secured in the same way as the calico, ensuring that any pattern is straight and centred.

Bottoming Measure across the underside of the seat frame from the outer edges of the rails from side to side at the widest point and from back to front. Cut a piece of bottoming to this size on the straight of grain, adding 2.5cm (1in) all round for allowance. Turn under allowance all round the bottoming so that the folds are 5mm (2in) from the outer edge. Tack centrally in place, placing the 13mm ($\frac{1}{2}$in) tacks about 2.5cm (1in) apart. Replace the seat in the chair frame.

UNSPRUNG SEAT

Webbing Attach the webbing to the top of the seat frame as for the drop-in seat, slightly splaying out the webbing if the seat is wider at the front.

Hessian Position and tack the hessian in place over the webbing as for the drop-in seat.

Filling Place the filling under the bridle ties as for the drop-in seat, building up to one-third higher than the intended finishing height of the seat.

Scrim or hessian cover Measure from one side of the seat rail to the other side of the seat rail over the filling at the widest point of the seat. Measure from back to front in the same way. Cut a piece of scrim or hessian to these measurements following the straight of grain. Mark, using a pencil, the centre of each rail and the centre of each side of the scrim (hessian). Temporarily tack the scrim (hessian) in place at the front and sides matching centre points. Cut the scrim (hessian) into Y shapes to go round the back struts. Temporarily tack the scrim (hessian) in place at the centre back.

Through stuffing ties These ties anchor the filling firmly in place. Thread a double-ended needle with a length of twine and push through all thicknesses one-third of the way in from the back and left-hand side edge. Bring it back, eye first, 2.5cm (1in) away. Make a slip knot (Fig 1). Repeat to form a square of

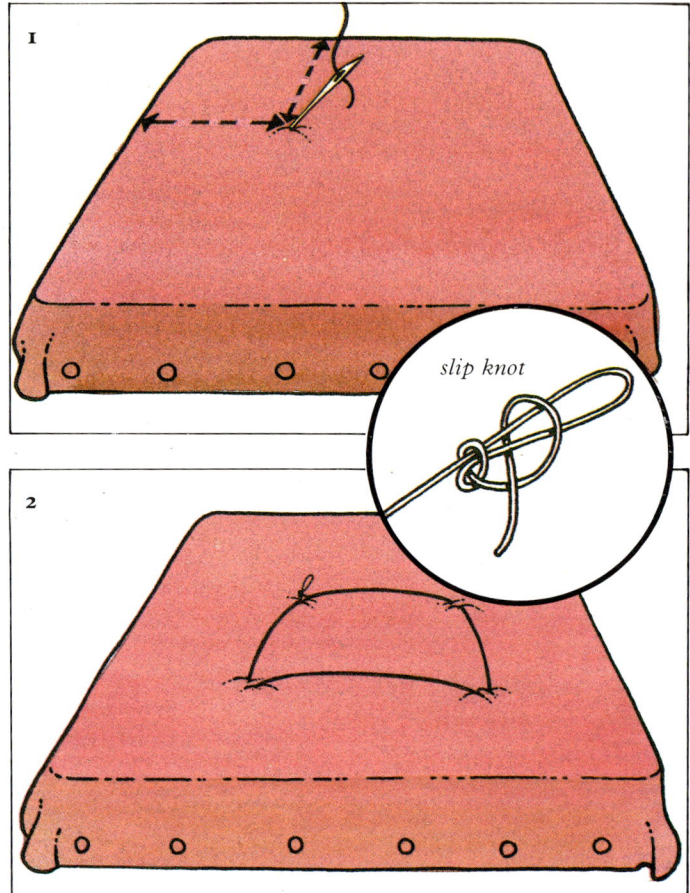

slip knot

knots about 2.5cm (1in) in the centre of the chair (Fig 2). Remove the temporary tacks and even out the filling, adding more if necessary to protrude beyond the edge of the chair frame. Now, turn under the edges of the scrim (hessian) and temporarily tack in place to within 2.5cm (1in) of the corners. At the front corners, push the excess scrim (hessian) in towards the middle of the chair legs and tack. Fold in both sides and tack in place. At the back, turn in the edges down both sides of the chair leg and tack in place. When the shape looks good drive home all the tacks.

Blind stitching This stitching anchors the filling in place between the centre and the rolled edge. Mark a line, using tailors' chalk, one-third of the way between the seat edge and the through stuffing ties. Begin the stitching at the back in the left-hand side of the seat. Thread a long length of twine on a double-ended needle. Insert the unthreaded end of the needle 5cm (2in) in front of the left-hand back strut just above the tacks. Push the needle upwards at an angle of 45° and practically out of the scrim (hessian) at the marked line. When you can see the needle's eye, replace the needle into the filling again and bring it out 2.5cm (1in) at the same level it went in but 2.5cm (1in) nearer the back corner. Pull through and tie to the main length with a slip knot, pulling it tight. Repeat this action, but when the needle comes out of the scrim twist the twine hanging in a loop below the needle two to three times round the needle. Pull out the needle, pulling the resulting knot tight (Fig 1). Continue in this way all round the chair seat. Keep the stitch line straight and just above the tacks, being careful not to place a twisted section round a corner. Finish with a firm knot.

Rolled edge The rolled edge will make a good firm edge which will stand up to years of use. It is similar to blind stitching, but the needle is pulled through on the top of the filling to enable a stitch to be made on top. Mark a line using tailors' chalk, 2.5cm (1in) in from the rounded edge of the scrim all round the edge of the seat. Thread the double-ended needle with a long length of twine. Begin in the same place as the blind stitching, but about 4cm (1½in) above. Insert the needle into the filling vertically and out at the marked line. Re-insert threaded end about 2.5cm (1in) to the left of this point, keeping it parallel to the first entry, so it will emerge 2.5cm (1in) away. Tie the end of the twine with a slip knot. Insert the needle again and complete the stitch, placing it about 2.5cm (1in) to the left, so it falls short of the first stitching. Before withdrawing the needle, wind round the twine as before (Fig 2). Continue round the seat, finishing with a firm knot.

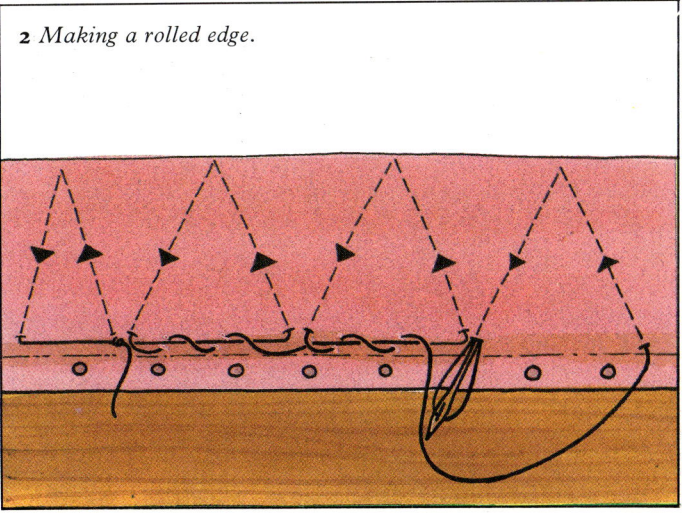

2 *Making a rolled edge.*

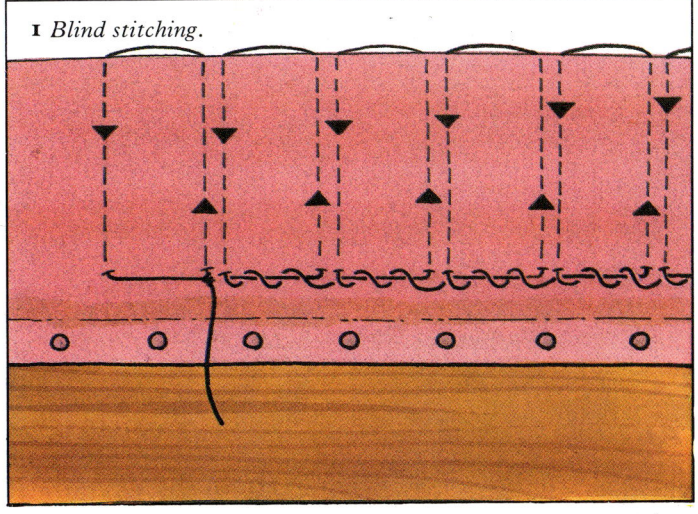

1 *Blind stitching.*

Second filling This second layer of filling should fill in any indentations which have been formed by the rolled edge. Make four bridle ties round the centre stitching. Place a small amount of filling under each bridle tie.

Wadding Measure and position wadding to seat as for drop-in seat, but cut into the back corners so the wadding will fit round the back chair struts.

Calico Measure from the bottom edge of one side seat rail to the bottom edge of the opposite seat rail at the widest point. Measure in the same way from back to front. Cut a piece of calico to this size following the straight of grain. Using a pencil, mark the centre of the chair rails and the centres of the calico. Place the calico centrally over the wadding, matching the pencil marks. Cut into the calico at the back corners to fit round the back uprights. Temporarily tack the single calico at the back, 2.5cm (1in) from the bottom of the seat rail. Pull the calico forward to the front of the seat and temporarily tack in place. Either make a double pleat at the front corners or an inverted pleat. To keep a smooth look to the seat, pull the calico hard over the rolled edges. Be careful to keep the calico grain straight. When the calico looks good hammer the tacks home.

Top cover The top cover is attached to the chair in the same way as the calico, through a single thickness of fabric. If there is a pattern remember to centre the pattern when cutting out and placing on the chair.

Finishing off If the cover is attached to the front face of the frame the raw edge of the fabric and the tack heads are covered with braid, stuck in place with fabric adhesive. Mitre the corners of the braid where necessary.

Bottoming Cut and position the bottoming as for the drop-in seat.

SPRUNG SEAT

Webbing Measure and position webbing as for drop-in seat, but place the webbing on the underside of the seat to accommodate the springs.

Springs Stand the springs in an upright position on the webbing in a square on top of the webbing intersections, with the beginning and end of each spring towards the middle of the seat. Each spring must be secured in place, beginning with the right-hand spring.

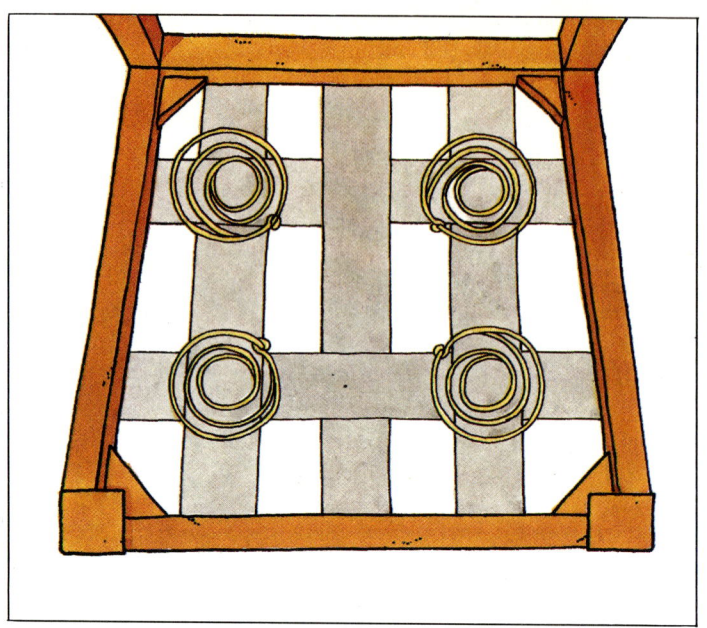

Thread a half-circular needle with twine and push the needle through the webbing from the underneath close to the outside edge of the bottom coil, leaving a tail of twine underneath. Insert the needle into the webbing again from the top catching the bottom coil of the spring with a stitch. Knot the twine to the tail. Move to the opposite side of the spring and stitch in place again in the same way, then repeat at the back of the spring. Move to the next spring and repeat. Continue until all the springs are in place. Fasten off firmly.

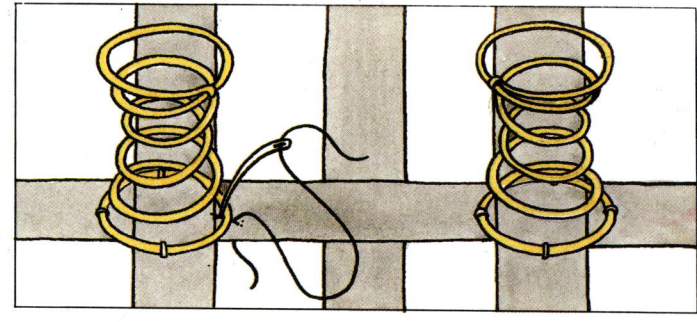

Lashing the springs This will keep the springs in an upright position. Measure over the top row of springs and cut a length of laid cord twice the length to tie down the springs in that row. Attach two 15mm ($\frac{5}{8}$in) improved tacks to all four sides of the frame, each one in line with the centre of a spring, and hammer halfway into the frame. Leaving a long tail of cord, tie the cord round the tack on the back rail and hammer the tack home. Take hold of the longer length of cord and while depressing the spring with your hand to two-thirds of its normal height tie a half-hitch to the second coil down on the first spring. Then tie a half hitch on to the top coil at the opposite side of the same spring. Carry on to the second spring in the row. Tie a half hitch to the top coil of the second spring at the side nearest to the first spring. Then tie a half hitch to the second coil down on the same spring. Wind the cord from the last spring round the tack on the front rail at the same time depressing the springs as before. Hammer the tack home. Take the short length of cord and tie it back to the top coil of the nearest spring pulling tightly so it leans down towards the frame. Secure each row of springs in the same way.

Hessian cover Measure from the outside of one side of the seat rail, over the springs to the other seat rail and add 5cm (2in) to this measurement. Measure from back to front in the same way and add the same allowance. Cut a piece of hessian to this size, following the straight of grain. Place the hessian centrally over the springs, making sure that the fabric grain is straight. Turn up the 2.5cm (1in) turnings all round. Using 13mm ($\frac{1}{2}$in) fine tacks secure the double-backed hessian to the seat rails, placing the tacks about 4cm ($1\frac{1}{2}$in) apart and making neat folds at the corners. Keep the hessian taut.

Stitching the springs Stitch the springs to the hessian in the same way as to the webbing, but make a slip knot at each stitch to keep it firmly in place.

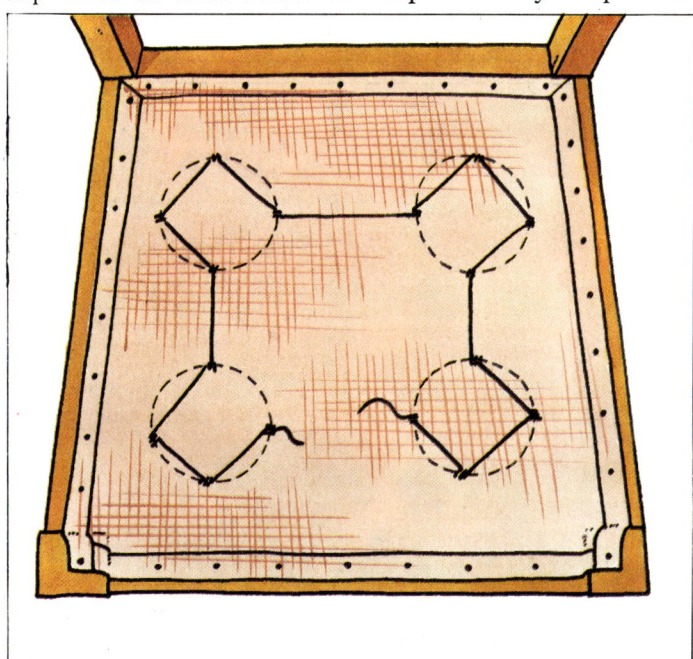

Once the springs have been sewn in place, work the remainder of the sprung seat following the instructions for the unsprung seat, starting with the bridle ties.

Larger seats and sofas are upholstered in the same way as these three methods, but on a larger scale.

'Textile' is the term used to cover all embroideries, tapestries, samplers, cloths and lace as well as the different kinds of fabrics used in household furnishings, from curtains, tablecloths and bedlinen through to carpets, rugs and upholstery. Unlike modern fabrics with convenient care labels telling you how to clean them, old textiles offer no such information, presenting quite a different set of problems from their new equivalents. Thanks to air pollution caused by industrial waste, light, the passage of time and general wear and tear, all textiles over about twenty years old have to be treated with caution and care.

Frankly, DIY cleaning methods are not advisable on antique textiles (technically speaking items over one hundred years old). When it comes to valuable or particularly fragile items, this narrows the age to around fifty years or so. Slightly damaged heirloom samplers, tapestries, Persian rugs, Kashmir shawls and the like are best repaired by experts; poor work could spoil irretrievably and permanently devalue. You must assess your own ability over things of lesser value. Generally speaking, unidentifiable old stains, and the cleaning of large bulky, lined articles is a job for experts.

The best thing to do if you suspect you own anything really valuable by the way of textiles, is to visit, or send good photographs of it to, the Textile Conservation department of a museum with a costume gallery or specialist interest.

A GENERAL GUIDE TO CLEANING, STORAGE AND DISPLAY

Tapestries, carpet and beaded embroideries and furnishing fabrics with a nap such as velvets and moquettes need careful handling, and the same goes for fabrics with a special finish, e.g., glazed cotton chintz, watered moiré silks – or anything hand-painted. Moiré silk markings, for instance, are made during the printing process with special rollers and washing would remove these. Old glazed chintz finishes are also removed in washing, but there are firms who specialise in re-glazing. If you plan to re-dye an old fabric, check first to see it is not faded. Old velvet curtains streaked from the sunlight cannot be simply redipped another colour (see page 49). Some professional dye firms will not accept faded curtains or furnishings of this type unless perfect, and suggest dyeing faded and streaked fabrics black or navy.

If possible, do all patching, darning repairs to broken seams, removal of rusty fasteners etc., *before* cleaning and pressing. Patching repairs camouflage more successfully if you do them beforehand. If you can see a spare piece of original fabric so much the better, otherwise the next best alternative is to use a similar piece of fabric. If it is new wash it several times and tint or dye it as near the same colour as the background, using the appropriate sewing needles and threads. Professional invisible menders use threads taken from an unobtrusive seam on the fabric. Do not use sewing machines to darn or patch old fabrics; not only do repairs look obtrusive, machine stitches may damage delicate fibres and cannot be undone. Couching stitches on a suitably coloured nylon net is the technique employed by conservation experts for protecting old tapestries and petit point. Irremoveable stains are better left untreated or in the case of non-valuable items, camouflaged by 'motif patching' or by painting out with fabric paints. Embroidery and beadwork repairs should be done using an embroidery frame and correctly matching up threads and beads.

CLEANING

Start by vacuuming Place a piece of nylon mono-filament over flat items and vacuum through; a hand-held attachment is necessary – car vacuum cleaners are also ideal. Beadwork should be cleaned with an artist's sable brush, taking care to get dust out of crevices.

Washing is generally voted the best policy when it comes to dirt-removal, but care should be taken to check that colours are fast. Make a test beforehand by dampening a corner or a seam before placing between two sheets of clean white cotton or blotting paper. Press fabric firmly, and if no colour appears then it is probably colour-fast. In the case of embroideries and patchwork quilts, however, it may be necessary to carry out this colour-fast test on every section. Certain reds in prints on white cottons can be notoriously unstable; blacks and blues can be tricky, too, so always test first. Use soft water at cool temperatures for hand washing; water softeners can be added but can make whites go yellow. Rinsing of any old and fragile textiles should be done with distilled water as this prevents future iron-mould spots forming. Buy distilled water from a chemist, not a garage. Remember, very hot water may harm wool and linen and never

rub at soiled areas or use harsh detergents or bleaches. A spirit soap, soap jelly or bran wash (see page 47) is safest on delicate, faded prints and embroideries. Wet washing embroideries, woven tapestries and petit point (including Berlin wool work) may not always be satisfactory. Canvases have often been treated with a water-soluble size so water may remove this and may also shrink the canvas. Embroidery containing metallic threads may tarnish almost immediately and beading threads may break. Either dry-clean using one of the methods described below, or if in doubt have the item professionally dry-cleaned by specialists.

Any moisture extraction should be done by blotting – never squeezing or wringing. Dry flat. Items such as lace can be pinned out on a piece of soft (insulation) board covered with clean white terry towelling, or dried flat against glass. Never dry in direct heat or sunlight – this is too harsh on old fabrics and may cause more fading and yellowing.

Dry-cleaning may be used when fabrics cannot be washed for some reason, i.e., if non-fast, too fragile or liable to tarnish.

Warm potato flour heated in a double saucepan can be spread on the surface of a textile; the heated flour should pick up a certain amount of surface dirt but should be brushed off before it cools.

CARE, STORAGE AND DISPLAY

Old embroidered or antique patchwork quilts and bedspreads should never be left on occupied beds, even if it is just an overnight stay! Heirloom spreads like these should be carefully rolled up and stored in a clean cotton drugget. This should be used to cover the same spread during the daytime. The same goes for old, delicate upholstery fabrics, which should be covered with clean cotton druggets; the use of a simple loose cover is a practical idea, and one a good many stately homes still employ.

Dust and dirt are not the only enemies of old textiles; sunlight, fluorescent lights and certain spotlamps beaming directly on to something can cause irreversible fading. Textile conservationists suggest keeping blinds and curtains drawn whenever possible, and avoid handling old textiles. Fingerprints are acidic and can do immense amounts of damage. Curtains in old and delicate fabrics may be difficult to protect in the same way if in use, as may cushion covers of old and delicate fabrics.

Old tapestries will need backing on suitable fabrics. A net lining has more stretch 'sideways' so this is placed lengthways on to the textile. Large lock stitches are used along the lines of greatest strain. Suitably coloured net is also used to cover delicate and worn tapestry and upholstery areas using couching stitches to secure. Industrial width 20mm ($\frac{3}{4}$in) Velcro or Nylon pile tape running the full length of top and base is sewn to the back of a hanging; more tapes may have to be used at frequent intervals on the backs of large hangings. Corresponding Nylon pile tape (hook

side up) is then fixed to wall-fixed battens.

When it comes to framing small pieces of lace, embroideries and beadwork, make sure that picture glass does not touch the textile surface. A filet (use wooden beading) must be made to hold the frame away – in the same way as framing for pastels and chalk drawings. If the piece is very old and fragile, care must be taken to see that the fabric background and adhesives do not harm and cause a chemical reaction.

Generally speaking, all textile storage should consist of rolling fabrics around cardboard rolls, which have been wrapped first with acid-free tissue – this prevents any harmful chemical reactions from the cardboard. Storing small items flat in acid-free tissue and lining drawers with the same will help keep items clean, uncreased and prevent deterioration.

Special fabric spray-on treatments exist for protecting fabrics against dirt but their use is not recommended; these may darken colours, and alter textures, and their long-term effects are not known. The same goes for insect repellents, although Mystox solution against moths is sometimes used. Fray preventatives containing ethyl alcohol are useful on badly fraying silk. Although areas treated may become slightly stiff, items can be washed or dry-cleaned afterwards and colour change is slight. Often hitherto delicate embroideries on cushion covers can have an active life again.

IDENTIFYING THE FIBRES

You may have to become something of a textile chemist yourself to find out what a particular textile is made of. Fortuitously, most old textiles will be made of one of the natural fibres and, therefore, comparatively easy to identify. The difficulty comes when textiles are lined and interlined with various fabrics needing different cleaning methods. This is a job for experts, as it usually involves unpicking the whole article and cleaning each part separately.

COTTON

Fibres are derived from the seed heads or bolls of the cotton plant. There is greater heat-resistance in cotton than in other fibres, although sunlight causes weakness and yellowing of white cottons. They are stronger when wet but in the case of old cotton fabrics, care over bleaching has to be taken. Old printed cottons, e.g. cretonnes, and cottons used, say, in old patchwork quilts may present colour-fast problems and may need to be dry-cleaned. Bran washing (see page 47) prevents colours fading and bleeding to some extent. Buckram curtain pelmets and bump interlinings are also made of cotton and need dry-cleaning rather than washing as special finishes would be affected. Collectable cotton textiles can range from special embroidered tablecloths and pillowcases and sheets to glazed chintz loose covers and curtains. Velvet and plush fabrics, lace and chenille, can also be made of cotton.

Test: Cotton burns steadily when near naked flame; water dropped on cotton will stay on the surface before absorption.

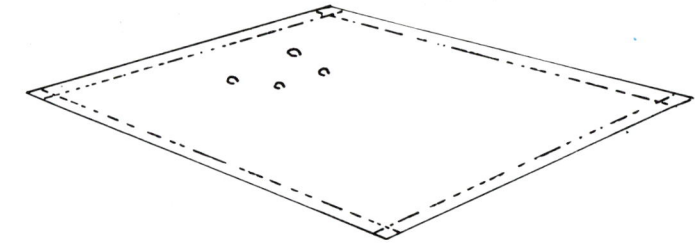

WOOL

Wool retains its original properties as a protective covering long after processing; namely the power to absorb up to one-third of its own weight in water without feeling damp. Fibres favour damp conditions and will eventually decompose under strong sunlight. Wool is liable to attack from moths and mildew and will 'felt' in very hot water.

Wool in the antique mode is generally seen in Kashmir shawls, tapestries and rugs. Persian and Indian rugs, of course, need to be repaired professionally, although some wools may colour-match quite well. Real goathair binds Persian carpet edges, and this is available from specialist craft shops and suppliers. Delicate and valuable carpets should not be trampled underfoot but displayed on the wall, out of direct sunlight as this affects colours. Persian rugs are originally washed in soft-water mountain streams to deliberately fade colours, but if home-washing avoid soaking for longer than ten minutes without checking dyes. Always dry carpets and tapestries flat. Small rugs and carpets can be treated in the bath but larger carpets should be professionally dry-cleaned, as the average home lacks the space, storage and equipment needed. Old faded Chinese carpets can be dyed with carpet dyes very successfully, but again this is a laborious job on large carpets, so it is best to have this done professionally. Felt fabrics and Numdah rugs cannot be dyed, or washed for that matter, so must also be dry-cleaned. Wool must never be soaked or bleached.

Test: If fibre is burnt with a naked flame it will smoulder with a characteristic 'damp feathers' smell and stop burning when flame is moved, with the fibre forming a blackened, charred knob.

SILK

Silk is the natural thread of the silkworm and used in its protective cocoon in the pupa stage. Fibres are less elastic than wool. In the manufacturing process the gum-like sericin that holds silk threads together in the cocoon is removed. The loss is restored sometimes with metallic salts resulting in 'weighted silk'. This is very difficult to wash, as in the case of fringes and tassels. If ironed it should always be on the wrong side with a cool iron. Never soak or bleach.

Silk was woven on jacquard looms in brocades, for curtains and upholstery, embroideries and hangings – oriental varieties are fairly fragile and 'shatter' when

old and worn; it also frays easily so old curtains etc., are best not left to hang too long. Taffeta silk is used in some antique furnishings; moiré for instance must be dry-cleaned or water marks will disappear if washed. It responds to treatment with fray-preventatives; damaged silk embroideries can be backed with iron-on adhesive interfacings, but these are not suitable for free-hanging silk curtains. Old embroidered silk items such as cushion covers and bedspreads can be very fragile. Never wash as colours may run and attempts to resuscitate are rarely successful. Repair silk embroideries with silk threads.

Test: Smells like burning hair if it comes into contact with a naked flame.

LINEN

Linen derives from fibres of the flax plant and retains moisture well. It is stronger when wet rather than dry and can be washed or dry-cleaned successfully.

Irish linen is the best known and turns up in table accessories, embroidered chair backs, tea cosies, table cloths and bedding. In its pure state it has a tendency to crease so modern linens are often blended with another fibre. Linen unions used in furnishing fabrics are exceptionally hardwearing, but finer linens are used in samplers, embroidery work, drawn thread work, white work, etc. Iron while damp – on the wrong side for a matt finish, on the right side for a shiny finish. Linen thread is available for darning, patching etc., from specialist craft shops. Fine linens respond well by gently manipulating when drying, which is the best way to treat fine embroideries, and samplers. Avoid ironing, even at the lowest setting, as heat could damage fibres.

Test : Drop water on to linen – it will spread and be quickly absorbed.

WASHING

Old textiles were never the aggressive, harsh whites we know today, although aniline dyes, first introduced in Victorian times were glaringly harsh until more control was gained – Berlin wool work being a case in point. Despite this, it is best to acclimatise the eye to yesterday's more subdued colours. Old cottons, silks and linens with so-called white backgrounds may look cream or grey to us and for this reason new embroidery threads and ribbons make them look dingy. The answer is not to use harsh modern bleaches or detergents to whiten. Hydrogen peroxide can be used successfully, but in the long-term interest it is best not to overdo this whiteness obsession. Old laces were never that white anyway; more verging to-wards creams and gingery browns. These shades can be successfully tinted back by soaking in tea or coffee, and faded colour, as in the case of Persian carpets, is part of the intended design even if it is uneven. If you own one where that has happened and looks exaggerated in one particular area, turn or move the carpet, wallhanging or rug at regular intervals so light can reach other areas.

To dry clean cream or white shawls, spread on a clean sheet and powder generously with powdered starch, or magnesia. Fold the shawl, adding more powder to each layer. Wrap a sheet around and leave overnight or for several hours. Take out of doors before shaking or brushing out all the powder.

OLD REMEDIES

Soap jelly Equipment: an old pan, knife and a board. Shred some left-over scraps of toilet soap finely. Put these into the pan and cover with water. For large quantities use 100g soap to 50.8kg water ($\frac{1}{4}$lb to 1qrt). Place pan on a gentle heat and allow soap to dissolve slowly. This soap jelly can be used in the washing of wool, silk, laces, or any material which will be injured by rubbing. Soap jelly gets its name because when cold it forms into a stiff jelly. To prepare quickly, put a piece of household bar soap into a jug, pour on boiling water and use some of this solution. Alternatively, use a nail brush to rub down sufficient soap into warm water.

Bran washing This helps to preserve faded colours and is suitable for most washable fabrics, particularly chintz, crewel work, cretonnes, as well as canvas and fur. Bran is the outer wheat husk; it contains a substance which cleanses fabrics, as well as vegetable and mineral salts to preserve colours. It also contains a starch to stiffen fabrics.

Use a fireproof casserole or enamel saucepan (bran corrodes metal) and measure 1 part bran : 4 parts water. Heat, and when mixture comes to the boil simmer for a further half hour. Strain through a fine strainer or muslin into a basin, then return bran mixture to the original container and add water to make the same amount as before. Divide this into three portions. Use two for washing and one for rinsing. To this bran water add an equal quantity of hot and cold water to make the solution lukewarm.

To wash with bran water add enough soap jelly to make a lather. Very little is needed as bran makes water very soft. Squeeze fabrics lightly in this. If necessary use a second wash of bran water, then rinse well, first in tepid water and then in plenty of cold.

Stain removal Old cottons and linen soft furnishings may have iron or rust marks caused by curtain fittings such as rings, and weights; loose covers and cushions may have hooks and snap poppers that have caused marking. Remove this and refit with Velcro (nylon pile tape). Staining can be removed on fabrics, provided they are strong enough, with a dilute solution of oxalic acid, available from larger chemists. Do a spot test first on a corner or seam. Oxalic acid is powerful and very poisonous. Throw away any leftover solution after use. Dilute as follows: 1 teaspoon of oxalic acid crystals to 600ml (1 pint) of hot water. Mix in a ceramic or rustproof bowl as metal containers will corrode. Tie stained areas with a piece of thread to prevent spreading and soak stains for 2–3 minutes. Rinse thoroughly in cool water. For fragile fabrics try lemon juice on iron and rust stains. Leave 10–15 minutes and repeat again if necessary before washing in concentrated suds and rinsing.

Mildew is a fairly common stain found on old cottons and linens. If it is fairly recent, washing several times in heavy duty detergent and hot water, then drying out in the sun, may remove. Old mildew stains may respond to soaking in a dilute solution of household bleach – 1 teaspoon to 300ml ($\frac{1}{2}$ pint) of cold water. Rinse the items well.

METALLIC TRIMMINGS AND TEXTILES (NOT EMBROIDERIES)

Upholstery gimps, braids and trimming fabrics become soiled and tarnished after a time but that does not mean that they cannot be freshened up. Just squeeze fabrics gently in a basin of lukewarm water in which Lux has been dissolved. Be very careful not to rub, as this would twist the threads. If fabric is very dirty repeat the squeezing in a second wash of soap flakes, then rinse at least three times in clean tepid water to remove all soap.

To dry, first roll items in a towel, squeezing out as much moisture as possible before placing on a clean, dry towel or sheet and stretching into shape. Allow to dry before an open window or in a warm room, but not before a fire. When nearly dry, press braids with a cool iron on the wrong side.

Metallic, striped and patterned textiles may also be washed in the same way, but these require to be stretched slightly while ironing.

In storage metallic fabrics and trimmings are likely to turn yellow or tarnish unless precautions are taken. Therefore, cover with acid-free tissue. Avoid touching metallic threads with finger tips as this will re-tarnish.

METALLIC UPHOLSTERY AND DECORATIVE TASSELS

Silver trimmings may respond to dry bicarbonate of soda brushed well in and left for an hour, and brushed off with a wire suede brush.

For gold trimmings, try a mixture of cream of tartar and dry breadcrumbs applied dry and brushed on and off lightly with a soft brush (e.g. old toothbrush).

CAMOUFLAGE – SEWING REPAIRS

Rips and tears in otherwise perfect old curtains, cushion covers and upholstery samplers can be treated in the following ways:

Iron-on adhesive webbings Opinions are divided about their use on old, valuable textiles – the main objection being that irreversible techniques should never be employed. However, iron-on webbings can be removed on washable textiles by soaking in cold water. The main objection to using them on fine silks and cottons is that the hang and fall of, say, a curtain could be spoilt. Iron-on adhesive interfacing can be quite successful as a backing to worn, frail embroideries and samplers with slight tears – these come in colours so can be matched to a particular background.

Patching The most sophisticated form of concealing blemishes can be achieved by treating the patch as part of an intended motif, or to blend as part of the printed or plain design. Some examples would be appliquéing silk motifs on to a fabric; raw edges can be over-locked by machine stitching or by hand – or

handsewn or bonded with double-sided iron-adhesive webbing. Lace medallions and edgings can be used in the same way – again any raw edges should be finished in the same way. Expert textile conservationists take endless trouble – some go as far as dyeing a piece of patching fabric to match a background so that the patch will blend in unobtrusively. The secret of 'Patch Camouflage' is to match the exact fibre, colour and weight, e.g., old Jap silk to old Jap silk and to sew with silk thread. Fabric grain in patches is also important; unless otherwise indicated, the straight of the fabric should always be used.

Painting out Small spots of, say, irremoveable gloss paint on a patterned background can quite simply be painted over using fabric paints. Mix up a little in the required colour and use this sparingly to cover, or make the mark look part of the pattern. Fabric paints and pastels can also be used to brighten areas of old net and lace curtains; also chairbacks, tablelinens and cushion covers of Richelieu work. Ironing with a cloth makes them colourfast.

VELVET

Faded textiles, in some cases, can be revived with powdered alum in the rinsing water, but if faded areas are patchy, as in velvet curtains, this will not be successful. Colour-stripping with special dye is the only lasting answer to dealing with faded velvet curtains. They will then respond well to re-dyeing with another colour in the washing machine, but curtains must weigh no more than about 2kg (4½lbs), half the average washing machine's washload. Larger curtains will need professional treatment as interlinings and linings will cause problems for home-dyers. Dust on antique velvet upholstery can be removed by gently vacuuming – again through nylon monofilament squares. When washing old velvet handle as little as possible, use warm water and dunk pieces up and down in the suds – *never* wring. After rinsing hang up to drip-dry. Older, more fragile pieces may have to be dried flat. To bring up the nap on tired and creased velvet, hang in a steamy atmosphere – the bathroom is ideal or else just above steam from a kettle. Panne velvet has a pile combed in different directions so, of course, must not be ironed. Moquette used in upholstery must be dry-cleaned. Chenille curtains and tablecloths respond well to delicate handwashing in liquid detergent, but dry flat and, again, do not iron. Holes and tears can be repaired with chenille yarn.

LACE

There are many different kinds of lace. Even if your lace is new, treating carefully can do no harm.

Delicate, smallish pieces of lace can be washed in a wide-necked jar into which pure soap has been diluted in warm distilled water. Put lace inside and shake for a few minutes; change water if necessary after 20 minutes. Pin out to dry on a board covered with white terry towelling using stainless steel (rustproof) pins. Very fragile small lace pieces should be tacked between pieces of white net or lawn using large couching stitches and placed in a flat plastic tray. Soak in distilled water for a few minutes then cover with nylon monofilament and sponge gently through lace using a natural sponge.

Sometimes dry-cleaning may be the only resort for cleaning very fragile examples. Cover these with magnesium powder and leave for ten minutes or so; brush or blow powder off. Repeat several times if lace can stand it. Methylated spirit in final rinsing water (distilled water prevents iron mould) brings up the gloss in silk lace; for cotton lace, however, a mild solution of household starch is effective. Never use spray-on starches on any old textiles.

Fragile lace is never ironed but eased back into shape whilst wet – dry wet pieces against a sheet of glass or plastic-surfaced cloth (PVC) stretched over soft-board and fixed with brass or stainless steel pins.

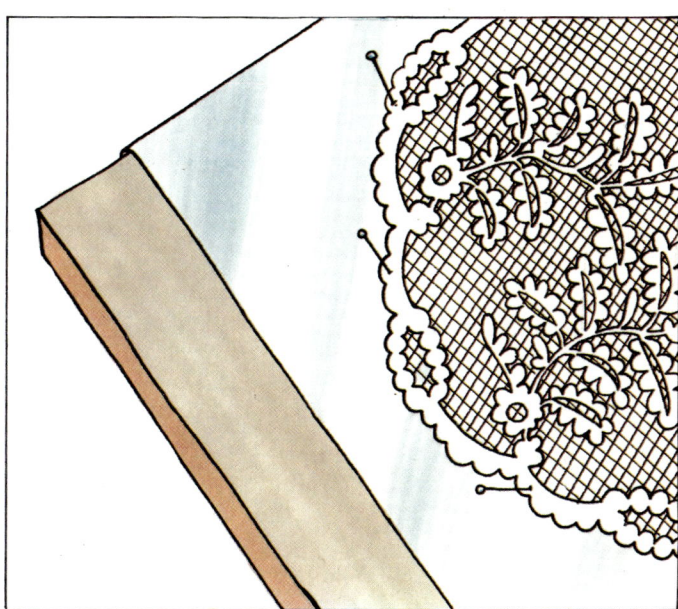

Lace and net panels for wedding veils, curtains and bedspreads may also have to be professionally cleaned if they are large and fragile, as the average home is usually without the equipment needed to tackle this kind of job.

CHINAWARE – CARE AND CLEANING

Prevention of breakage or damage is much easier and more satisfactory than repair, so do everything possible to preserve your chinaware.

Wash chinaware in a plastic bowl, using hand hot water and a bland soap powder. Avoid any cleaning abrasives, bleach, or soda. If acids such as fruit juice or vinegar are left on plates and dishes after a meal, rinse these off as quickly as possible before the decorated surface is damaged. Wash egg off with cold water to avoid it setting.

Egg stains or food that has been burnt on china can usually be removed by soaking thoroughly in hot water, and gently and persistently scraping with a finger nail. Tea or coffee stains on the inside of cups may be effectively cleaned off with a damp cloth that has been dusted with bicarbonate of soda.

When washing chinaware, use a cloth or a very soft brush. Never rub hard over decorated or gold-rimmed areas. Stand each piece separately in a rack to dry. After drying, the surfaces can be protected from marks by applying a little liquid silicone polish.

TOOLS AND MATERIALS

There is no need, certainly not at the outset, to spend money on sophisticated tools. Indeed, most of the essential items required can be found in your house or garage. Improvisation is the keyword here, and some people will obviously prefer to use different tools to carry out the same job. Provided your tool is effective for the purpose required, the scope is vast. It is really surprising how often you will find that many items you already have and frequently use can be adapted to help you with these jobs. In all cases, the type of work to be done will dictate the need. Many useful tools and supplies of excellent materials are contained in the numerous DIY repair kits which can be bought at quite modest prices.

The following are some items to start your own basic tool kit, and also materials which you will find very useful: small tweezers (eyebrow pluckers are ideal); long nose pliers; spring type clothes pegs; hacksaw blades; nail file; single-sided safety razor blade; an old toothbrush; wet and dry paper; sellotape or PVC tape, preferably in a dispenser for easy handling; plasticine; cocktail sticks; small square of glass or a glazed tile; magnifying glass; epoxy resin adhesive with its hardener; and acetone. Nail polish remover is acetone with an oil additive. This can serve your purpose if only small quantities are required.

Two other very useful tools are old dental probes and cutting forceps, sometimes obtainable from a friendly dentist.

When working with your tools make sure that they are kept clean at all times. Always keep a container of methylated spirit or acetone handy, so that tools can be kept free of paint, dirt, or adhesive. A sticky tool can give you a lot of extra work.

REPAIRING CHINAWARE

Many items are improved by repair. On the other hand, some dedicated collectors and antique dealers are horrified when they see a 'botched job' or new features introduced that were not on the original piece.

In some cases a damaged vase can be more valuable than one on which additions of moulding, handles, or colouring that are out of its period or style, have been introduced by the repairer.

If you have a piece of chinaware that is particularly cherished or has a high value, it makes sense to first seek expert advice before attempting any repairs yourself. A dealer specialising in ceramics or an auction house adviser will tell you immediately whether this is something you can deal with yourself, or should leave well alone and give the job to a professional repairer. You can usually get the name and address of one from your local antique shops.

On the other hand, if a broken or chipped item offends you, and the piece of chinaware is not particularly valuable, go ahead. Provided you observe a few well-defined rules, there is no reason why you cannot carry out your own repairs quite satisfactorily. Five fundamentals for success are: patience, a steady hand, good eyesight, adequate light, and suitable support for the repaired pieces.

When undertaking repairs, the ware of which the piece is made will influence the work, as will the tools to be used. For example, a very fragile vase or dish will need extra care with its treatment. When repairing or restoring a cherished and highly decorated piece, special vigilance must be observed to make sure that the surface does not come in contact with any form of abrasive or other material likely to injure the highly sensitive colouring. Once this has been damaged, it is often very difficult to restore.

SUPPORTS AND PROPS

Some people find it easier to mend a piece on their lap and then move it to a support, but there is a great deal to be said for carrying out the repair while the piece is already in a support. Once a piece has been mended with adhesive it is far better to allow it to dry in situ. Any slight tremor of the hands while moving it can displace the repaired part and weaken the adhesive.

Whichever method you choose, however, it is essential that the repaired piece is allowed to dry in an adequate support. It is a matter of common sense that if a plate is broken in half and then joined, the join will be weakened by the force of gravity if that repaired plate is allowed to dry in a horizontal position. Thus, a support or prop on which to stand the plate is needed so that it dries in a vertical position. If a handle of a jug or cup is repaired, the piece must be allowed to dry by being supported at an angle, rather than standing upright.

One method is to put the piece in a drawer, and then close the drawer on it to hold it in position. The

bottom of the piece can be securely held by pressing it into a layer of plasticine, or into two blobs of plasticine, one at each side.

A box or some other container with sand in it can be used to support pieces standing at an angle. The piece is pressed firmly into the sand and held secure. This type of support is used mainly for smaller pieces such as cups, saucers, and jugs.

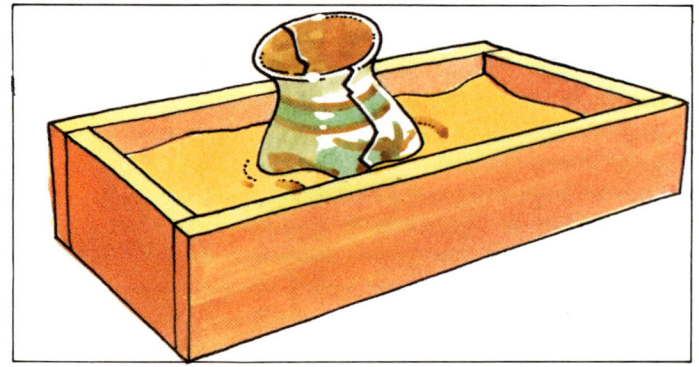

A repaired piece can be supported at an angle by pressing it into a base of plasticine.

Plate racks, draining racks or large toast racks can be used to support plates, dishes and saucers. Also, parts of an old orange box can make a very effective support for flat pieces like plates and dishes. The piece can be secured at the bottom by pressing it into a blob of plasticine at each side.

Pliers with the handles held tightly closed by a rubber band can be another useful support. Pieces can be made more secure in some supports by clamping them to the support with spring type clothes pegs. Sellotape, or PVC adhesive tape is very useful to strap the piece and hold the join until the adhesive is properly set.

MENDING A MINOR BREAK

When a plate, dish, or saucer is dropped and breaks into two pieces, it is quite a simple and straightforward job to join them together again.

Try to carry out your repairs on a firm surface, with space to assemble your tools and materials. If possible work in daylight and ideally in a room with northern light. A warm atmosphere will help the adhesive to set, and in cold weather it is a good idea to bring in an additional heater or use an electric light bulb that gives off heat. Decide which type of support you are going to use according to the size and shape of the piece on which you will be working. Make sure your support is set up before you start.

First, thoroughly clean the two pieces by soaking them in hot water with a bland soap powder. Ideally, you should use de-ionised or distilled water if either is available.

When the pieces are dry, clean the edges with cotton wool soaked in methylated spirits. If the break is a recent one, the edges will be suitably rough, but if not, carefully roughen them up with a nail file so that the adhesive will have maximum effect.

There are many adhesives suitable for repairing chinaware. For very small items such as miniatures and potlids, any proprietary instant drying clear glue is quite satisfactory. This glue can also be used on glassware.

For larger pieces, such as plates and dishes, however, an epoxy resin adhesive is most effective. This can be bought under proprietary names such as Araldite from suppliers.

Epoxy adhesive is normally supplied in two packs –

one containing the adhesive itself, and the other the hardener or catalyst with which to mix it. Usually the mixture is half and half, but full instructions are given on the packs. It is essential to use epoxy adhesive if the repaired piece will come into contact with high temperatures, although a brown stain will often appear around the join if the piece is subjected to intense heat.

Put the pieces together *before* applying any adhesive, to make sure they fit, and examine the edges with a magnifying glass. Any ridges that appear should be carefully filed down or rubbed with emery paper.

Now mix the adhesive with its hardener according to the instructions on the pack. Use a palette knife or cocktail sticks to mix, and avoid handling the adhesive. As there is a remote possibility that epoxy resin can cause dermatitis or other type of skin irritation do not take any chances. Ordinary rubber gloves are not thin enough for this job, but disposable surgical gloves that fit tightly will give your fingers quite a sensitive touch.

To bond the pieces together, apply a very thin layer of adhesive; the thinner the layer, the more effective it will be. Carefully wipe off any surplus adhesive with a cotton wool swab soaked in methylated spirits or acetone. It is essential to make sure that the edges of the join are clean, since once this adhesive has properly set, no solvent will touch it.

If you are repairing ornamental china or a piece not likely to be frequently washed in hot water or put into a heated oven, alternative adhesives such as nitro-acetate or cellulose acetate glues, which are quick drying, can be used. For earthenware repairs, a polyester resin glue will suit the purpose. Acetone is a solvent for cellulose glue.

Carefully press the two pieces together, hold for about ten seconds, then quickly release them to dry in their support. Once the adhesive has been applied, it is risky to hold the pieces for long, since even a slight trembling of the hands can weaken the bonding.

Lightly dust the join with French chalk. Leave the repaired piece to set in its support for at least twelve hours. If you wish, the setting process can be speeded up by placing the piece near a fire or a stove. Once the adhesive has set, clean the surface around the join by swabbing with cotton wool soaked in hydrogen peroxide. This should be handled with care.

REPAIRING A MULTI-BREAK

This is for mending chinaware that has broken into several pieces which are of various sizes and shapes.

Carefully fit the pieces together, making sure that they are all complete. Once you are satisfied that all are in their correct positions, temporarily strap them together with sellotape.

If there are more than two or three pieces, make a rough sketch of them as they are assembled, numbering each piece in its correct order.

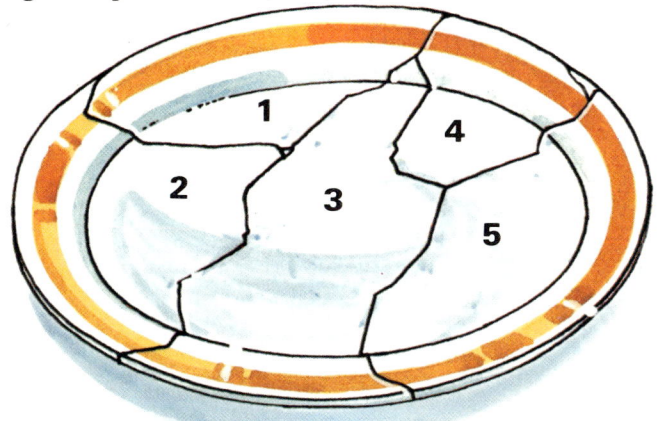

In some cases, and very frequently, several pieces are similar in size, but of course, each one will be slightly different. By making a sketch on a sheet of paper, you can be sure that when you bond all the pieces together they will be in their right sequence. Not only that, if you have to leave the job for a while to do something else, when you return it will be quite simple to join each piece in the right order.

Separate the pieces again, and thoroughly wash them in hot water with a bland soap powder. When they are dry, clean the edges of each piece with cotton wool soaked in methylated spirits.

Apply a thin layer of adhesive and bond the pieces together in easy stages. Start by bonding two pieces first. When these have thoroughly set, continue with the next two pieces and so on until the repair is complete.

RESTORING AND IMPROVING BADLY REPAIRED PIECES

It often happens that the beauty of an attractive piece of chinaware is marred by a clumsy and perhaps rather ugly repair or restoration. Old glues often leave a yellow or brown stain around the edges and sometimes this cannot easily be removed with hot water soakings.

During the last century it was popular to repair plates, dishes and vases with rivets. Not only do these often spoil the appearance of the piece, but they can leave unsightly marks where they are joined.

To remove rivets and old glue, wash the piece in hot water with a bland soap powder, and leave to soak for twelve hours. Rinse, and then, if necessary, repeat the process.

In many cases, soaking in hot water will loosen the rivets and also any old glue that remains. Try to prise the rivets apart with a probe or an old knife blade. Once the rivets have been loosened they can usually be extracted with small pliers. If they remain quite tight, however, and prove to be obstinate, cut the rivets with cutting forceps or saw them through with a hacksaw blade. Green stains so often left by copper or brass rivets can usually be removed by rubbing them with a swab of cotton wool soaked in ammonia.

If the old glue is not water soluble, you will have to move it with a solvent. There are several of these, but unless you can identify the glue, solvents will have to be used on a trial and error basis. Common solvents are methylated or surgical spirit, acetone, carbon tetrachloride and the various paint strippers.

First, dab the glue with cotton wool soaked in a solvent. If the glue does not respond, try immersing the piece in more solvent. Most of the old glues can be broken down with one of the solvents mentioned above, but make sure that the original solvent is thoroughly cleaned off the piece before you apply another one.

Once you have treated the glue with a solvent, carefully try to move it by starting at its edge, and working with a probe or your finger nail.

Plaster of Paris was often used as a filler to cover small holes at the end of rivets. This can be taken out by chipping with a probe or a piece of stiff wire. Any old paint smears left on the piece can be removed with paint stripper.

When the rivets have all been taken out and the old glue and surplus filler completely cleared, wash the piece in hot water and thoroughly clean the edges with cotton wool soaked in acetone.

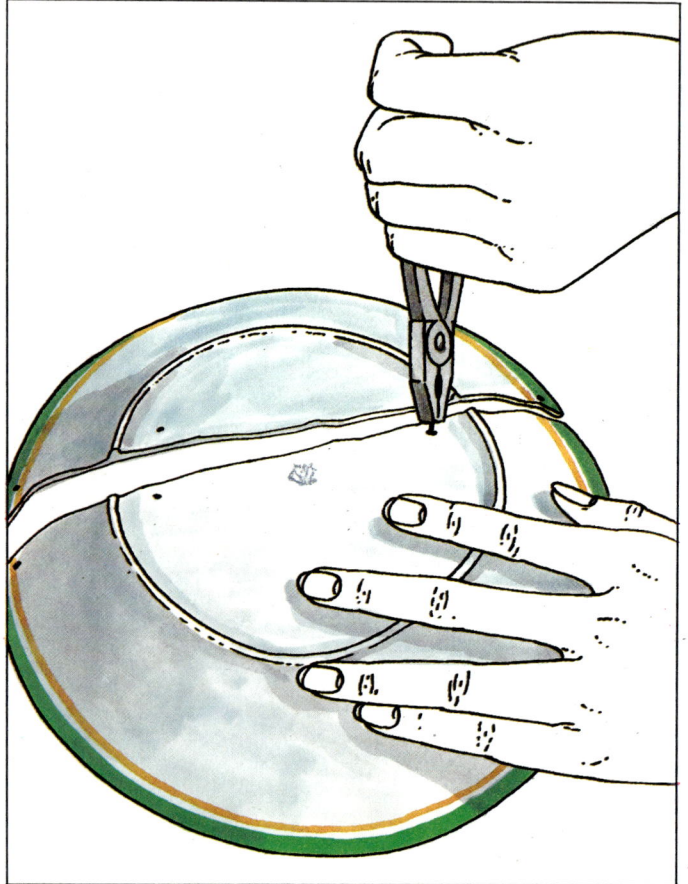

Once you are satisfied that the surface has been restored to its original condition, bond the pieces together in the usual way.

DEALING WITH CRACKS

Cracks are caused by ingrained dirt or by damage. Dirt cracks are usually quite superficial and should be moved fairly easily.

Swab the crack thoroughly with cotton wool soaked in a solution of hydrogen peroxide and allow to stand for twelve hours. Clean off with methylated spirits when dry. If the crack is still visible, repeat the treatment until it has been completely removed.

Cracks caused by damage must be repaired. Wash the piece thoroughly in hot water and a bland soap powder. When dry, clean the crack with acetone or methylated spirits. If it is quite shallow, rub down with wet and dry paper and touch up with paint or gloss. Should the crack be a deep one, restore the surface with a filler and touch up.

FILLING CHIPS AND HOLES

Many old pieces that were chipped have been clumsily restored with a Plaster of Paris filler which has now begun to flake off. The effect is not very elegant and it is worthwhile doing some restoration here. Holes, too, have often been filled in a similar manner.

Thoroughly wash the piece in hot water with a bland soap powder, and leave to soak for twelve hours. Rinse and dry.

Remove the old Plaster of Paris filler with a probe or knife blade and smooth the surface with wet and dry paper. Clean the area with acetone or methylated spirits.

Fillers are provided in most DIY repair kits or you can make your own with a mixture of epoxy adhesive and Kaolin powder. The Kaolin can be worked in to your liking and this filler has the advantage of not being too sticky and, therefore, easy to handle. If you wish, colour can be added to the filler before using it, and this often helps the final matching with the original colour.

Apply the filler in separate thin layers, allowing each layer to dry before adding the next. Gradually build up the layers until they are slightly above the level of the original surface. Smooth down with a knife or scalpel, and finish off by rubbing with wet and dry paper.

COLOURING REPAIRED PIECES

Fortunately the majority of repairs do not need painting to any extent. Generally, it is only where pieces have been chipped and coloured lines or surfaces destroyed that it is necessary to continue those lines or fill in some colour to match the original.

It is very difficult to match colours on chinaware, particularly when pieces are fairly old. Frequent washing and wear have combined to produce their own particular shades.

For most pieces, enamel paints are quite suitable. If the surface is a glazed one, the enamel will blend quite easily. Household pieces in quite frequent use with food must, of course, be coloured with harmless paint that has no lead content.

Mix your colours on a piece of glass or a glazed tile and try the results on white paper. Paints, brushes, and glazes are all supplied with DIY kits and there are full instructions for use.

Unless you are lucky enough to match the original colour right away, the only alternative is to experiment until you find one tolerably near the original. Whites are often very hard to match. Blue mixed with white increases its intensity, while a red mix gives it a warmer appearance. Work on the primary colours, red, blue and yellow; darken with black and lighten with white. A few guidelines on mixing are: red and yellow = orange, red and black = brown and so do red and green. Red and white = pink, black and white = grey, blue and yellow = green and blue, green, and white = turquoise. If in doubt, consult a colour chart.

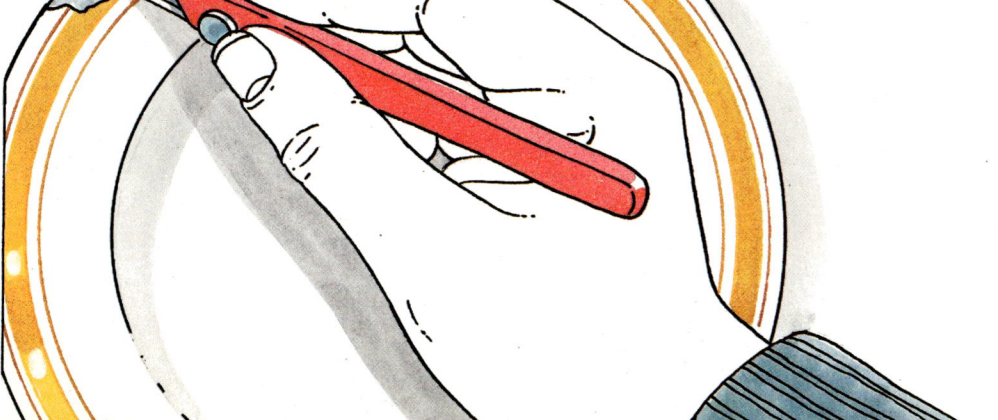

GLASSWARE

The art of glass making has been known to Man since at least the time of the Egyptians, but interestingly techniques for making coloured glass were discovered long before it was known how to produce clear and colourless glass.

The main ingredient of glass is silica, which is obtained from a wide variety of natural forms (e.g. sand, flint, quartz etc.) found all over the world. When heated to a very high temperature the silica melts to form glass. Natural impurities in the various silicas produce different tints. Early glass makers discovered that these could be neutralized by adding various chemicals, such as nitre, manganese or arsenic, but they were unable to achieve very precise control over these additives which often produced tints of their own. Thus, old glass is found in a very wide range of colours.

Modern technology has enabled manufacturers to consistently produce clear and colourless glass which can then be coloured. At the end of the 17th Century, an English glass manufacturer, George Ravenscroft, added lead oxide to his glass which made it especially brilliant. This is known as lead crystal glass. Different glass manufacturers throughout the world tended to develop their own techniques, which enabled them to produce their own distinctive type of glass.

The various shapes of glass are achieved by it being blown and pressed or moulded. It can then be etched, or cut and polished or even sand blasted. Not only can it be coloured but also one colour of glass can be overlaid on another to produce many artistic patterns.

Most modern household glass is either potash or soda glass. There are, however, various other glasses which have special properties, i.e. are heat resistant or unbreakable or inhibit the passage of ultra-violet light (Crookes glass).

Glass is a very versatile substance and has found a wide variety of uses. Its decorative qualities have made it a very collectable item, and some pieces are extremely valuable. If you have a piece which you suspect is valuable, it is advisable to obtain an expert opinion about its worth, and leave any repairs to professional restorers.

CARE, STORAGE AND DISPLAY OF GLASS

Despite it being a very hard substance, glass is very brittle and therefore care should be taken when handling it. The better quality the glass, the more fragile it becomes. Because of its high lead content crystal glass is particularly prone to shattering or being chipped.

Somewhat surprisingly, glass is also prone to deterioration if subjected to excessive dampness or humidity. This is particularly true of glass manufactured before the 17th Century. Therefore, when storing glass it should be kept in the driest place possible. It should not be wrapped in tissue or other paper as this would encourage the accumulation of any dampness in the atmosphere.

It is not a good idea to store decanters with the stoppers in place as they may become stuck and be difficult to remove. If this should happen do not attempt to force the stopper out by severe twisting. Instead, try pouring a small amount of methylated spirit together with a few drops of olive oil or glycerine round the entrance of the decanter. Leave overnight before trying to remove the stopper again. It should come out quite easily, but if not, try a few *gentle* taps to help release it.

CLEANING GLASS

If glass has become really dusty it is better to wash it rather than try to dust it, as fine particles of grit among the dust could cause scratching. If possible wash each piece of glass separately, in hand hot water containing a little detergent. You can rinse the object in cold water but if it is old and fragile rinse it in luke warm water to avoid subjecting it to sudden changes in temperature. If left to drain, the glass may become 'water spotted', so it is advisable to gently dry the piece with a soft linen cloth or soft chamois leather. Do not use a cloth which would leave pieces of lint on the glass.

Some articles, such as decanters, have a very narrow neck which makes it difficult to dry inside the vessel. These can be drained upside down overnight to remove most of the moisture and then dried with a large piece of soft cloth, such as a tea-towel, inserted inside. Alternatively, a hairdryer can be used to dry the inside of an awkward shaped piece, but ensure that the heat is not too severe to cause damage to the glass.

Glass is prone to staining which can result from actual deterioration of the glass, or may result from residues of, say, wine being left in a decanter or glass.

One method of removing stains is to fill the vessel with warm water containing approximately one teaspoon of vinegar. Leave overnight before draining and washing as previously described.

There are also various proprietary stain removers available which are quite effective, but always follow instructions for use carefully.

Persistent stains can be removed with a dilute solution of 5 per cent nitric or sulphuric acid. However, *extreme caution* must be observed when using any toxic substance; always wear rubber gloves and make sure the decanter or vessel is repeatedly and thoroughly rinsed out before use.

REPAIRING GLASS

As glass is transparent it is virtually impossible to disguise a break since, when repaired, the light catches the broken edges like cut glass. The edges are also thin and smooth which makes adhesion difficult. However, the techniques for repairing glass are similar to those employed for repairing china and porcelain.

Carefully wash and dry the pieces to remove any grease, then assemble them in order before beginning to stick them together. It may be necessary to hold the pieces in place with adhesive tape stuck on the inside of the object.

There is a wide variety of adhesives available which can be used for repairing glass. Some will stain the glass more than others. Epoxy resin adhesives give a strong bond but are dangerous to use and need a steady hand. Always follow the instructions for use carefully.

It is important to give the adhesive plenty of time to work so do not attempt to move the repaired piece too soon. Like everything else, it helps if you can practice on some unwanted piece before tackling a special object.

The stems of glasses are particularly vulnerable to breaks and these are easier to mend. Clean the broken edges as above, but before applying the glue prepare a cradle or mould for both ends of the glass so it is not disturbed whilst the adhesive is drying. The mould can be made out of any pliable material such as plasticine.

Man has been using metal in one form or another for thousands of years. Metals can be divided into two groups, natural and man-made. The natural metals found in the ground are gold, silver, copper etc. The second group are called alloys, which are mixtures of various combinations of natural metals. Brass, pewter, plate and Britannia metal are such. The more modern materials such as chrome plate are amalgams of man-made alloys. Alloying hardens the natural metals and changes their colour.

Extreme care must always be taken when cleaning and repairing metals. The state of the piece and its value must always be borne in mind. Never rush into cleaning. If in doubt about age, the local museum should be able to help. Never hesitate to take advice when offered by an expert.

GOLD AND GOLD PLATE

Gold is the most prized natural metal. Its colour is yellow, and it is easy to work. Copper is added for hardening and to increase resistance to scratching. The proportion of gold to copper is expressed in carats. Pure gold is 24 carats, but is rarely used today because of the high cost. Gold plating is 9 carat gold. Gold coins are 90 per cent gold and 10 per cent copper. As gold does not tarnish it is often used to protect other metals.

GOLD HALLMARKS

The ability to read hallmarks is very important. The presence of a hallmark is your guarantee of (**1**) the place where the piece was assayed, (**2**) the year it was assayed and (**3**) its quality.

The hallmark can be carried out only by an appointed assay office, and under strict rules laid down by the Goldsmith's Company. As London is the main assay office, it is useful to look at each of the goldsmith's marks in turn: A leopard's head will be seen,

this being the London assay mark. Next comes the maker's mark, always the last name first. Thirdly is the annual letter. This can be the most difficult to determine properly. The letters repeated over the years, but the shape of the shield containing the letter usually uniquely determines. All letters were used except for J, W, X and Z. Finally comes the head of the sovereign in profile, this being the duty mark, indicating that duty had been paid on the piece. George II faced to the left; George IV to the right. Queen Victoria, who faced to the left, was the last sovereign whose head appeared on the assay mark. After 1890 the sovereign's head was no longer used. On lower standard gold, 18 carat and 9 carat, the duty mark was omitted.

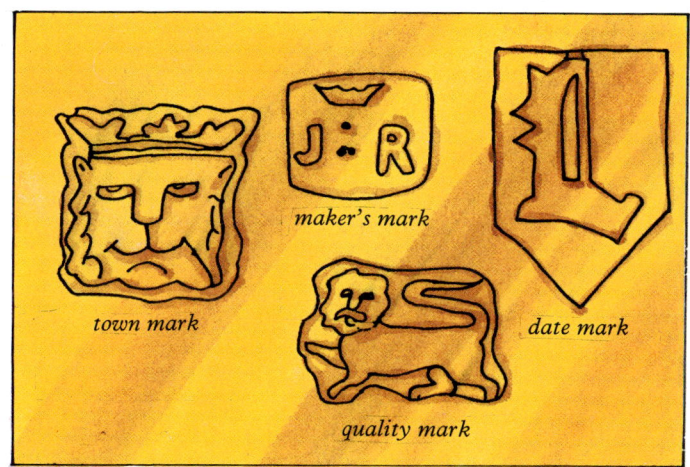

town mark
maker's mark
date mark
quality mark

Articles exempt from assay Although it is compulsory for all domestic gold to be assayed, certain pieces are exempt by virtue of their size, and if the mark would detract from the piece's appearance. Examples include such items as thimbles, pencils, bottle tops, wine labels, and snuff boxes if the gold is only decoration.

CLEANING GOLD

As gold does not tarnish very little needs to be done. Wash in gentle soap suds. Dry, and polish with a soft cloth to avoid scratching the surface.

A jewellery cleaning kit can be used for small pieces. A fluid is contained in a glass jar, which also holds a removable basket. Place the jewellery in this and follow instructions.

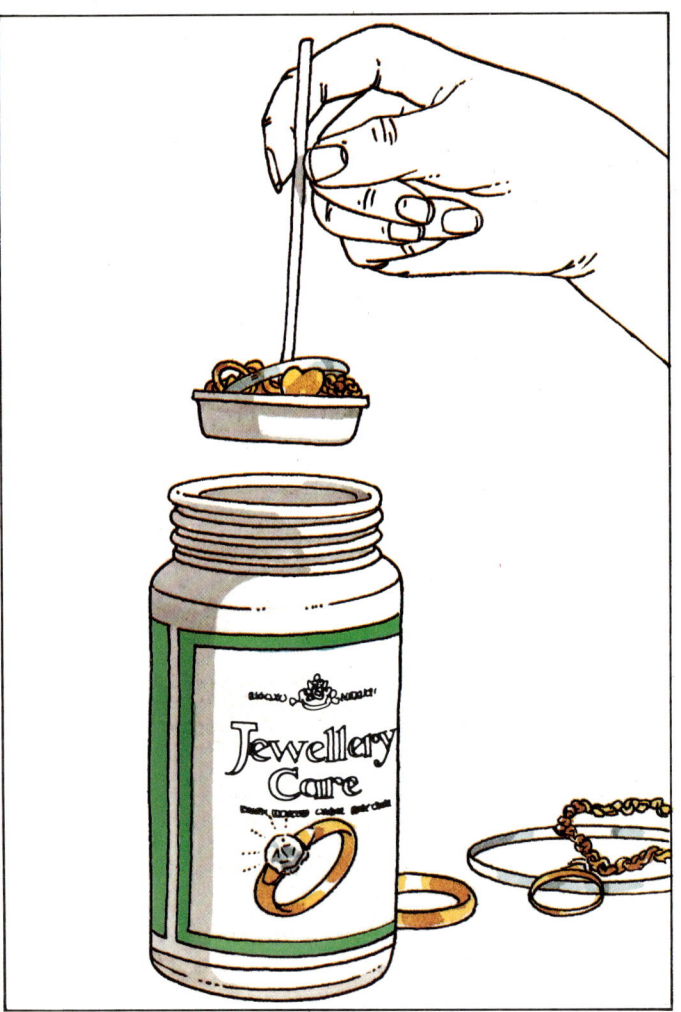

REPAIRING GOLD

This should not be attempted without experience. For those who wish to learn for themselves, many higher education colleges offer courses in shaping and repairing metals.

SILVER

Silver has long been used to make a wide variety of objects. At the small end of the scale there are chains, lockets, charms, bracelets, snuff and stamp boxes, card cases and vinaigrettes. Silver is also used to decorate tortoiseshell and ebony. It is used for all sizes of cutlery, called flatwear, candlesticks and every kind of table decoration, such as epergnes, centre pieces for flowers and salvers.

CLEANING SILVER

Wadding can be bought almost anywhere; liquid cleaner is also very good. Still obtainable is the pink block long used in stately homes.

If a piece is badly tarnished or spotted, silver salt will soften black spots; so will lemon juice. Leave on for a few minutes, and repeat if necessary. For inaccessible corners on engraved pieces an old toothbrush is useful. If the piece is not used regularly, keep in a plastic bag well toggled-up. Cover the hallmark when cleaning. A worn hallmark is hard to read and reduces the value.

SILVER HALLMARKING

Silver has the same format of hallmarking as gold. Sometimes the number 995 is added. Such silver is the purest of all. This means that the silver piece contains 995 parts of silver to 5 parts of alloy. Some older silver is 900 parts per thousand pure silver. This was the old standard silver content, and would be hallmarked. A small reference book listing hallmarks is a good investment and enables you to look up the age of each piece. As with gold, small pieces do not need to be marked, but mustard and salt spoons usually are if they are part of a set. Such marks are sure signs of the finest quality.

Watchpoints: Most pieces will be what they seem. However, there are certain items such as sugar tongs which are cut down to make teaspoons. In Victorian times tankards were changed to jugs and given as wedding presents. You may find a jug with additions by a local silversmith, a spout and a lid added to make it a teapot. Such items should be sent to be reassayed, but seldom are. In the trade these pieces are called marriages, and their sale is illegal. They are no longer genuine, and the whole value has gone. Only the scrap value remains. If such pieces come up for auction they will be withdrawn before the sale.

As with gold, do not attempt makeshift repairs. The look and value will be lost.

SILVER PLATE

Silver plate is copper sandwiched between silver skins. There are various types of silver plate. Sheffield plate was invented in 1740. It consists of copper sandwiched between two sheets of silver. A clear sign of wear is the copper showing through. It is often called merely British plate. The hallmarks are similar to silver. Beware.

Britannia standard silver can be identified by punchmarks and the seated figure of Britannia, a lion's head with a wavy neck, the maker's mark, the first two letters of his surname, and a date letter. The lion's head was discontinued in 1975.

Plate is used mostly for household items such as tea services, salvers, candlesticks and tankards as well as for small everyday Victorian trinkets such as scissors, sewing sets in boxes, grape scissors, candle snuffers and any small item a lady or gentleman might wish to have, but could not afford in silver.

CLEANING SILVER PLATE

Some caution must be taken. Silver dip must not be used as discolouration will result. Clean only with a product whose labels recommends use on plate. It can be brightened with Spanish whiting (blanco). This paste is good for silver as well. Finally polish with a soft cloth as before.

REPAIR OF SILVER PLATE

Not to be attempted by the amateur. If tankards and teapots are taken to be mended make sure silver is not used. It will be a different colour, and detract from the value.

Watchpoints: In good quality plate the copper shows through. This is thought attractive by many. Some people take off all the plating to reveal the copper beneath, depending on taste. Plate is best not cleaned too often as it will rub away and reveal the copper.

BRASS

Brass is perhaps everyone's favourite. It is an alloy, a mixture of copper and zinc. The colour usually tells the age. Older brass has a reddish glow, due to the high copper content. Brass has been used since medieval times, mostly for household items. Items that you might find today range from a simple candle box, to a hand-held candlestick, to an ornate candelabra; trivets for resting pans on by the hearth; and mechanical pot holders, called jacks, which could be wound up and down to prevent a hanging pot from burning. Brass was also used for making penknives, and desk pieces such as inkwells and pounce pots (a powder used to dry ink before the invention of blotting paper), as well as to decorate walking sticks, and for fire implements, guards and fenders. This leads on to novelty items: tobacco boxes, tobacco stoppers, often shaped like a boot. Then there are door stops and knockers, keys and padlocks.

CLEANING BRASS

Brass tarnishes quickly, especially if the atmosphere is polluted. When cleaning, the first rule is patience. The dirt has taken years to accumulate, so a little time spent removing it will not be amiss. Add some strong bleach to boiling water, stir, and immerse the piece. Leave for ten to fifteen minutes, inspecting occasionally. Beware of scalding. Cool in cold water before touching the piece.

If the piece is large carry out this cleaning in the sink. Exercise control over the water and use tongs to wrap old sheets or rags around. If still not clean after fifteen minutes, repeat. Wash in detergent and soda crystals, then polish.

TRIED AND TESTED RECIPES

Many people have their own recipes handed down by the family. Here are a few well-known ones.

Mix together 30 parts of oxalic acid and 100 parts of water. Always add the acid to the water, never the other way round. To this solution add 40 parts of 90 per cent proof turpentine and 40 parts of charcoal powder. This will now be a stiff paste when mixed. Taking a soft cloth, rub the paste onto the brass taking care not to leave runs. Avoid scratching.

A quicker method is to take half a lemon, dip in sea salt if available (sea salt is coarser than cooking salt) and rub over the piece. Any stubborn black spots should now disappear.

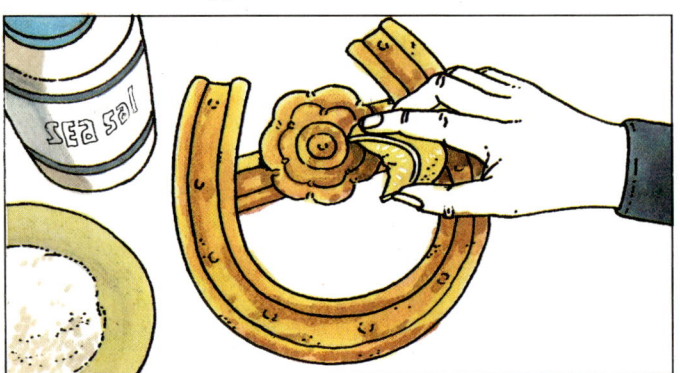

If cleaning a brass handle on furniture, it is important not to allow any of these solutions to touch the wood. Cut a template from cardboard and place it behind the handle as a safeguard.

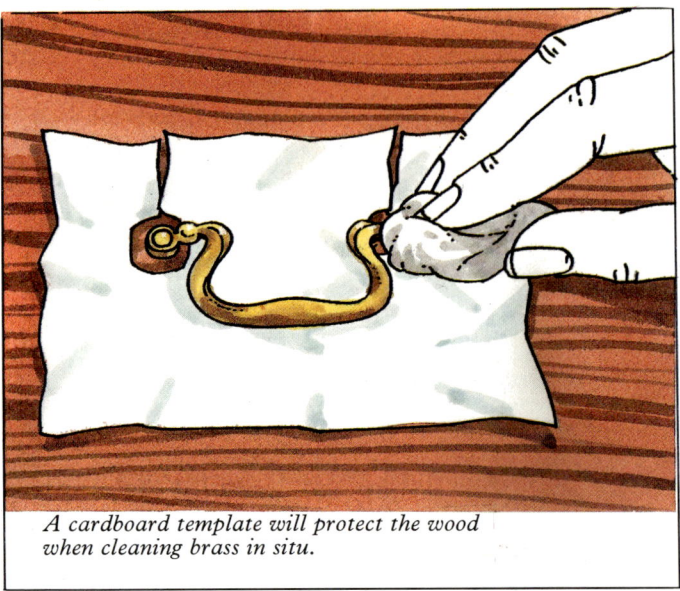

A cardboard template will protect the wood when cleaning brass in situ.

To keep their brass ornaments bright French and Spanish housewives often place their brass in the sun for a few hours in the hottest part of the day. This seems to fix the brilliance for a long time.

Experts disagree about lacquering for protection and there is some evidence that it may damage the brass in the long term. Given time, it is perhaps best to lacquer, especially if the brass is normally inaccessible on a high shelf or wall. Before applying the lacquer, rub over with white spirit, wearing cotton gloves to avoid leaving fingerprints. Alternatively, hold with a clean cloth. Any marks left on will show through the lacquer. A spray lacquer is the quickest to use, preferably outside on a windless day. If using a brush, apply in one direction for an even finish. Brush strokes do not matter as they will vanish on drying. Be sure to put in a dust-free place for drying.

REPAIRING BRASS

Best left to the expert. Dents must be carefully hammered out. Brass must be mended with brass.

Watchpoints : Of items sold today, brass reproduction output is very high. There is nothing wrong with this, but some people sell these pieces as originals. Beware of handles, joints and rivets.

COPPER

Although a natural metal, copper has zinc added for strengthening. Old copper was hammered from an ingot by hand. It was always uneven, and this can easily be seen on close examination. Also, the joints are always visible in old copper.

CLEANING COPPER

Methods for cleaning copper are generally the same as for brass, because of the similarities of the materials. Again, fixing in the sun will retain the brilliance once polished.

Another good method to brighten copper is to spread borax on a wet cloth or towel. Spread with a knife, add plenty of soap and rub the piece all over. Remember to clean from the bottom to the top to avoid runs. Finally, after drying rub into the piece whiting powder and polish.

PEWTER

Pewter is another artificial alloy, consisting of a mixture of lead, copper, zinc and antimony. Old pewter contained some silver. This gave it a dull grey look. As it is a soft alloy it soon shows signs of wear, which is why good early pewter is so rare and collectable. In the sixteenth century the pewter companies decreed that no pewter was to be repaired, and it was sold as scrap. Also, as it was in everyday use, style and fashion changed; so it was melted down and reused. Pieces that survived would soon lose their original brilliance, become coated with verdigris, and be discarded.

CLEANING PEWTER

Some collectors prefer not to clean, claiming that the patina of age adds to the pleasure of the article. Metal polish can be bought, but if there is heavy corrosion add 0.45kg (1lb) of caustic soda to 18 litres (4 gals) of water. Place a soft cloth or some canvas in the bottom of the container, boil, and immerse the piece, stirring continuously. This treatment may take some hours. Rinse with detergent, then polish. Next clean with a gentle abrasive such as pumice stone ground to a powder. Add a little paraffin and rub with a soft cloth. Remember, pewter is quite soft. A light oil will prevent it from corroding again. A quick way to get a glow on pewter is to rub in oxalic acid, pure or diluted. Prolonged soaking in paraffin will remove stubborn tarnish. Finish off with a metal cleaner. A short time in the sun to fix the surface will allow the pewter to keep its brilliance longer. For cleaning, hot beer rubbed in with a woollen cloth will remove any film on pewter. Vaseline is also excellent.

REPAIRING PEWTER

Filling of a hole or crack without soldering can be done with a two-part epoxy resin. This has limitations, as the colour may not be the same and it will not polish well. This can only be used for areas not generally seen.

BRITANNIA METAL

Britannia metal is an alloy of tin and antimony. Often called poor man's silver, it was used as a base for plating. It was despised for many years but is now collected as avidly as pewter. After 1850 a new stamp was used on Britannia metal, EPBM (electro-plated Britannia metal), with the full maker's name on the base, often with Sheffield added. There is no emblem. It became more popular and for a time replaced the more expensive copper.

CLEANING BRITANNIA METAL

Clean as for pewter. As for repairs, these alloys can be rivetted or soldered with the right tools, but these jobs are best left to experts.

CHROMIUM PLATE

Chromium plate consists of 18 per cent chromium and 8 per cent nickel mixture on the base metal. The process was perfected in the 1930s by William Wiggins of Sheffield. He was searching for a metal that could be used in bathrooms and other steamy atmospheres. Today chromium plate is widely used, and not only in the home.

CLEANING CHROMIUM PLATE

Do not use metal polish except one specially for chromium. Rub with a soft duster, and use silicone cream for shoes or furniture. If badly discoloured, wash with warm soapy water first, then polish. Steam will eventually cause the chromium to disfigure. A quick rub down after the bathroom has cooled can prolong its fine appearance.

STAINLESS STEEL

This is basically steel with chromium and other alloys added. It will stand up to much wear and tear without staining. Surprisingly, hot liquids will remain hot longer in stainless steel than in china or silver. The first stainless steel teaset was shown at the Ideal Home exhibition of 1934. As with most innovations, the public were slow to buy, preferring silver or plate. When hotels and restaurants discovered the great heat retention qualities of the new material its commercial future was assured. Today stainless steel products are common in every home.

CLEANING STAINLESS STEEL

There are many choices. There is of course a special wadding on the market. To remove stains from cabbage or other vegetables try bleach. Pour it on neat, and rub in with a piece of fine steel wool. Hospitals use methylated spirits to polish their stainless steel. Most spray polishes serve well, but they leave a film. Soapy water is often adequate, and silver dip is also safe to use.

RESTORING PICTURES

It is surprising the number of old pictures that have been passed down from generation to generation and, because they look dilapidated, have been consigned to the attic. If you have such a hoard it is well worth examining them closely. They may be unframed and tied up in a roll or already framed. Look for the signature of the artist, generally at the bottom right-hand corner, sometimes on the left and very occasionally at the top. If you can decipher it consult an encyclopedia of famous artists. If the signature has been cut off and, in your opinion, the workmanship shows signs of quality, take it to a reputable art dealer for advice.

Even rough preliminary sketches sometimes have considerable value; similarly old monochrome prints and steel engravings (which may or may not be hand-coloured in flat watercolour washes) can prove to be a good find.

WATERCOLOURS

Watercolours, so popular in the last century, will normally be painted on paper and protected from dirt deposits by glass.

Foxing Small brown spots often appear after a picture has been exposed for a number of years to a damp atmosphere. These marks are caused by mould and known as 'foxing'. If these are on a white surround, say, in the case of a vignette, you may be able to wipe them off with a cloth wrung out in water to which a little household bleach has been added. After the spots have disappeared, dab off gently with clear water and mop dry with white blotting paper. Experiment in an out-of-the-way corner first, supporting the picture on a sheet of glass, as you will not know of what the paper is made – rag, wood pulp or other material. If this 'spotting-in' process leaves white patches, as it may well do against a discoloured paper, you will have to touch them over with an off-white watercolour paint; as there are colour differences in paint in its wet state and when it is dry, owing to refraction, match up with a dab of paint that has dried. Fox marks in the middle of the painting may not be noticeable and you can only hope they will not spread – which they are not likely to when hung in a dry atmosphere.

If they show, touch in delicately with the same bleach solution and, after they have disappeared, dab off with a wrung-out cloth wrapped around the index finger, press on white blotting paper and mop dry. Then touch them in as well as you are able with a fine artist's brush. The spots are likely to be only a few millimetres across and your corrections, if not perfect, will hardly be visible.

In the case of a watercolour, or indeed a picture painted in any other medium, which you suspect to be of great value, it may be advisable to get an expert to do the job for you.

Tears in paper can be patched with acid-free tissue stuck on between the tear with wallpaper paste.

OIL PAINTINGS

As a rule oil paintings are not protected by glass because its reflective properties could cause distortion, detracting from the picture's merits. Instead, they are varnished, but this will not protect them from the darkening effects of dirt.

Remove the picture from its frame and support the canvas underneath on something solid such as a sheet of glass. As the varnish will probably be on a glue base, do not use water for cleaning. Just wipe over the surface lightly with white spirit, rubbing in with a circular motion – again lightly – with powdered rosin on the finger tips. Protect the fingers with a glove or finger-stalls. Stop rubbing when the rosin dust starts to change colour and specks of pigment appear just before the coating is removed, to avoid biting into the underlying glaze coat. Then wipe off with white spirit. Now revarnish. You can use a natural varnish such as Dammar or mastic, but as these are often difficult to obtain and also tend to yellow with age it is best to use an appropriate synthetic varnish.

Some artists use a flat knife or spatula for applying their oil colour instead of a brush, resulting in heavy indentations which are a trap for dust. These will have to be flicked over with a stiffish brush and, if obstinate, scraped out very cautiously with a finely pointed knife or scalpel.

RENOVATING PICTURE FRAMES

Highly ornate gilded picture frames lost their lustre in the course of time.

To restore them, first try turpentine applied lightly with a soft brush and then immediately mop up with a sponge. Do not use a detergent which could easily ruin what is left of the gilding.

If this is successful, the frames can then be kept in pristine condition by applying parchment size made by boiling scraps of parchment in water. This evens up the lustre and, when dirty, can be washed off and fresh size applied.

If a frame is very disreputable, with gilding peeling or dull beyond instant repair, there are various methods of restoring it.

A non-descript dark colour appears in the intricacies of the moulding of most gilded frames with brilliant gold on the prominent parts. To restore, paint the whole frame in a dark colour and, when dry touch over the high parts with finely milled gold paint. At least two coats will be needed to hide the dark colour completely. Finish with a coat of clear varnish.

The second method is to paint the whole frame in gold and, when dry, repaint the whole in the dark colour. While the latter is still wet, wipe over the protuberances with a soft cloth. This will show up the gold on the reliefs and leave the intricacies dark.

Renovating picture frames : First method

Second method

The third way, which is more laborious but imparts a near gold-leaf effect is to paint the low parts in the dark colour and leave to dry. Then brush the high parts over with a sticky varnish and, while the latter is still wet, gently rub in fine bronze dust. The rubbing-in action shows hardly any signs of the normal roughness of even the best gold paint because it forces the metallic particles into the medium and coats them over as well. If you cannot buy varnish of the right consistency, use ordinary varnish and allow its medium partly to evaporate. Then rub in the powder.

Chipped frames can be patched with a cellulose stopper, fireclay or gesso. To make your own gesso dissolve 50g (1oz) of animal glue in $\frac{1}{2}$ litre (1 pint) of water. Leave to soak for an hour. Heat in a glue pot but do not allow to boil. Add 100g (2oz) of plaster of Paris to get it stiff. Then add 50g (1oz) more of plaster of Paris and 50g (1oz) of hard wall plaster to get the mix stiff enough for modelling with a scalpel. When dry, paint.

HANGING PICTURES

If you are lucky enough to have picture rails round the walls of your rooms, these will enable you to change your pictures round at will without marring the wall surface. If there are no rails, use picture pins which may be obtained either single or double according to the weight of the picture.

Do not hang pictures over a radiator unless it has a shelf over it to deflect heat because, as hot air is lighter than cold, it will rise and carry dust with it. Most open fires will have a mantelshelf serving the same purpose as a radiator shelf. In any case, undue heat will do picture and frame no good.

Medium sized pictures can be hung with one length of picture cord over one picture hook. Large ones may require two cords and two hooks. In the case of very heavy oil paintings it would be safer to plug the wall in two places and use two lengths of chain. Although cord is very strong eventually if may fray and cause the picture to fall and be damaged.

RESTORING STONEWORK

You may already have sandstone or marble sculptured pieces which are chipped, broken or badly stained and need repair. If not, they can often be acquired cheaply at junk yards and from demolition contractors and second-hand shops. An occasional look through charity shops is also worthwhile.

Repair may seem a formidable task; but that is not so, provided you do not mind the time spent and have patience to exercise care.

EXTERIOR STONEWORK

When looking for items of exterior stonework it is best to choose those made of sandstone or marble. The former is likely to acquire a black patina, particularly if you live in a district with high industrial pollution. It is the only feasible stone to do extensive repair work on for outside projects, but beware as it is relatively soft. Being porous, it also soaks up rain which carries dirty fumes into its intricacies.

In the past it was customary to carry stone ornamentation very high up, right to the top of a building. Such ornamentation is now generally precast in concrete and let into a mock stone fascia. This comes very much cheaper than employing a sculptor to work *in situ* on a 'one-off' principle.

Attempts to brighten up older city buildings have, to a large extent proved abortive. Certainly clean stone is left but this exposes a fresh surface to the inroads of fume-laden rain which soaks in and, as the integrated ice expands it loosens more of the surface. If this cleaning process is continued, eventually there will be little stone left. Therefore, it seems better to leave the stone, for the coating of dirt acts in a way similar to that of a coat of paint; it seals the pores and protects the work from further disintegration.

For smaller items in a garden it is a good idea to give one clean only and then protect the surface from further harm by applying a colourless silicone waterproofing solution to reject dust which will otherwise soak in with rain and cause disfigurement.

An alternative is to paint the ornament with a product called 'Hammerite'. This gives it a hammered metal appearance which will hide the stone but the finish will remain brilliant and last for many years. Such treatment would be excellent for a statuette standing on a concrete foundation in a pond. If the piece incorporates a fountain, splashes of water will do no more harm than rain and, in any case, you are likely to turn on the fountain for a relatively short period only when entertaining friends.

Yet another alternative is the use of a stone-coloured smooth masonry paint. Using such materials will necessitate only one cleaning.

Articles attacked by moss and mildew can be treated with a special fungicide obtainable from builder's merchants.

Large buildings are steam-stripped by experts using expensive apparatus. You can achieve a similar effect on a small garden piece by wirebrushing, aided by steam from the spout of a boiling kettle. One problem is that you will have to use several kettles to ensure a constant jet while completing the job.

INTERIOR STONEWORK

Interior stonework, such as a bust needs cleaning only occasionally, particularly if protected by a silicon solution to repel condensation and dust sticking to the surface. Dust with a soft brush, but very gently so that the bristles do not bend and skate over the minute raised portions, leaving dirt behind in the crevices. Flick over the surface lightly, working backwards and forwards and in a circular motion. Wipe sparingly with a damp cloth, then leave to dry before applying a fresh coat of silicone. This will be needed each time after washing – which may be only every three or four years.

If the piece is broken, liberally coat the meeting edges with an appropriate adhesive. Make sure the pieces are adequately supported while the glue dries. If necessary tape the fine pieces in position with sticky tape. Specialist firms exist which supply such materials developed for repairing stonework. For hard ceramics use an epoxy resin. However if repairing soft stoneware such as terracotta or earthenware it is advisable to use P.V.A. adhesive. Epoxy resin adhesive might make a stronger job, but when the broken parts are pressed together, it would be more difficult to wipe off exudations and there would be a danger of too much adhesive soaking into the stone. A repellent could certainly be applied first, but this could form a weak joint so that the broken part would drop off again at some future date.

Chips can be stopped up with adhesive and a *stiffish* mix of one-and-four mortar, modelling to shape with a sculptor's modelling tool. Stir in a tinter (obtainable from good paint or artist's sundries shops) to match with the surrounding stonework. Tinters are better than powdered pigment which is more likely to change colour with the passage of time.

After the stonework has been washed and dried, apply a colourless silicone waterproofing solution which will help to repel condensation to which dust will stick. The solution will have to be renewed every time the piece is washed. In between times, just dust with a small clean paintbrush.

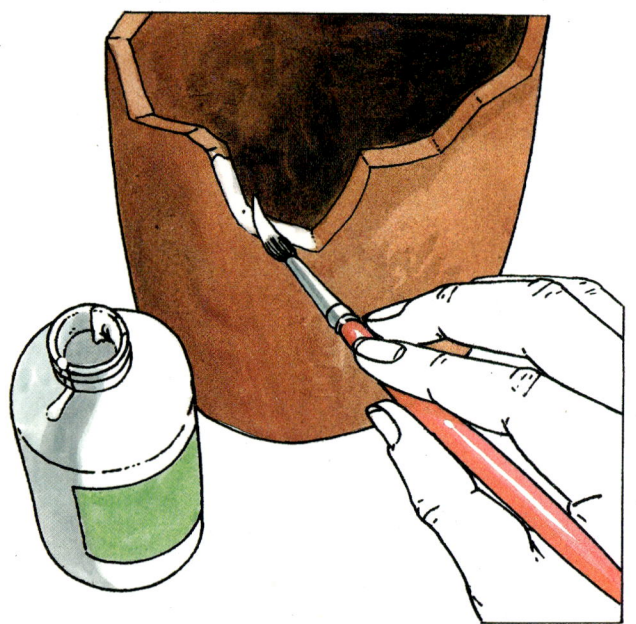

MARBLE

True marbles are divided into crystalline limestone with a granular structure and those that are not crystalline and capable of being polished. Both have various colours provided by impurities. The tints range between off-white (some are snow-white) which is pure and unadulterated by oxides, through all shades to black. Rosewood marble is so-called because of its resemblance to that wood when polished. White marbles are quarried in Paros, one of the Cyclades islands. It is called Parian marble and is the kind used by Greeks and Romans for their ancient statues and buildings.

The Parthenon is built of pentelic, from Pentelicus close to Athens, and is even whiter than parian. Connemara, named after the Galway town where it is quarried, is green and onyx and shows concentric rings of greenish yellow and brown. This is largely used for expensive challenge trophies and suchlike.

Another attractive marble is black owing to the presence of bitumen and has traces of green in it. It comes mainly from Connemara.

Marbles used in modern buildings are quarried mostly in Carrara, Italy.

All these share the same fault as sandstone in not weathering well, especially in cities.

There are also several manufactured marbles composed of marble dust and powdered limestone bonded with polyester resin and veined by the addition of pigments dragged through in process of manufacture.

CLEANING AND RESTORING MARBLE

Cleaning marble presents difficulties because stains soak in. 'Cutting' the surface below to the depth of penetration entails the use of an abrasive paper wrapped round a block of wood of convenient handling size. To reach the intricacies of ornamentation, crease the paper, rough side out. Then follow with a rubbing compound – the kind used in motor-car painting and obtainable at motor-accessory shops.

After this treatment, polish vigorously with a soft cloth.

If the stains are confined merely to the surface, try removing them with lemon juice or artificial denture cleaner. Then apply silicate of soda (from chemists and builders' merchants) to seal the surface and prevent the formation of future stains.

If marble is used for table tops and dressing table tops a copious supply of drip mats will always have to be at hand, as no alcoholic drinks or fruit juices should be stood directly on them.

CLEANING AND RESTORING SLATE

A relatively inexpensive substitute for marble is slate, used largely for mantelshelves. Until a few years ago this was dipped in a tank of water on the surface of which were floated coloured pigments ground in gold size, and blended by slowly drawing a stick through in various directions to form whorls and other patterns. The piece was then stoved.

This process produced an extremely realistic effect, but is hard to duplicate without the use of a large tank and equally large oven.

The reason for mentioning it is that, as the coating is of a paintlike consistency, it is likely to chip. If this has happened, and the chip is not too large, it can be touched up with a fine artist's brush and paint of the right colour.

Most people cannot be bothered to do this and often the mantelshelf is painted over. It is then an arduous job to remove the coating without injuring the simulated marbling underneath. Apply a spiritous paint remover on a soft pad, rubbing a few inches gently at a time. Examine frequently to make sure the marbling is not coming off. If you do make a mistake, touch in with a fine artist's brush.

Perhaps the most satisfactory way is to remove all the coatings and 'bring forward' to stop up any damage with a cellulose stopper. Then sand level with fine waterproof abrasive paper used wet, always rubbing in the same direction so that scratch marks do not show. In the case of a mantelshelf the direction would be longways, with the abrasive wrapped round a block of wood. Wipe off the sludge.

Take a handful of hemp or plumber's tow and dip it in a solution of shellac and glue. While still wet, tease out the strands to form a stencil of the pattern required. Leave to dry thoroughly and spray paint through it, using an aerosol containerised paint. When this is dry apply a coat of matt varnish followed by a glossy varnish.

Another way that takes more time and patience is to paint the whole in a matt background oil colour and

add scumble of the required tone on top. While the scumble is still wet, pick out the design you want with a pointed instrument. The idea of using scumble of one colour on top of a background of another colour instead of ordinary paint, is that oil paint tends to flow out whereas scumble stays put wherever the pointed instrument is applied. The last stage is to gloss-varnish over the top for protection.

It may prove difficult to obtain scumble from an ordinary paintshop because it was originally formulated for hand-graining doors and other room trim which is now unfashionable. However, as the process is still carried out to a limited degree, it can be obtained from a builders' merchant who supplies professional decorators.

When everything is dry, coat with varnish for protection of what is comparatively a soft coating.

Abrasive: substance or material used for removing unwanted coverings, e.g. metal polish, car paint cleaner, wire wool, sand paper, etc.

Appliqué: method of applying one fabric on to another, often in the form of a motif or pattern.

Alloy: man-made metal produced by combining two or more natural metals, or metal and another substance.

Batten: a thin strip of wood used for trimming purposes.

Bevel: type of edge which can be angled or sloping.

Beading: small strip of wood used as a decorative finish.

Britannia metal: modern alloy resembling silver.

Calico: type of plain cotton cloth used in upholstery.

Chintz: glazed, printed, cotton fabric with a stiff finish.

Cornice: ornamental moulding placed where the walls of a room meet the ceiling.

Cramping: method of binding things together (e.g. pieces of wood) by means of special devices called clamps.

Cretonne: heavy, patterned, cotton fabric used in upholstery.

Drugget: coarse, woven fabric.

Filler: any pliable substance which can be used to fill cracks, holes etc., e.g. plaster of Paris.

French polish: special high gloss finish for wood surfaces, consisting of shellac dissolved in alcohol.

Gilding: application of gold coloured finish.

Gesso: traditional paste made of whiting or chalk mixed with glue, used either as a filler or as a base for building up a decorative surface on picture frames etc.

Lacquer: a traditional yellow varnish giving a very glossy but often brittle surface.

Laminate: layers of material built up in strips for extra strength.

Hallmarks: special assay stamps embossed on some precious metals.

Hessian: inexpensive, coarse fabric made from jute; often used in upholstery.

Marbled: a swirly pattern applied artificially to imitate the stone.

Marquetry: small pieces of attractive wood laid in a pattern on top of a cheaper wood base.

Motif: a special design, often repeated, in or on fabrics, wood, metal, etc.

Moiré: fabric resembling watered silk.

Moquette: a heavy velvet used for upholstery.

Patina: an attractive finish on old wood or metal resulting from the build up of dust, ingrained dirt, and polish, over a long period of time.

Solvent: one chemical substance which dissolves another; common ones include methylated or surgical spirit, acetone, carbon tetrachloride, and paint stripper.

Stopping: to fill a hole or crack in wood, chinaware, etc.

Touchmark: assay stamp found on old pewter.

Template: pattern or gauge used as a guide.

Varnish: glossy, clear finish used to protect a delicate surface.

Veneer: thin sheet of attractive wood, or plastic, glued on to a groundwork of cheaper wood.

Woodworm: larva of small insect which tunnels through the wood, before emerging as adult insect via the familiar round woodworm holes.

List of suppliers

Nearly all the materials needed for restoration work can be obtained from local shops, or by consulting your Yellow Pages. For special items, or in case of difficulty, the following companies will generally supply by mail order. Most of them have catalogues, many containing lots of useful advice.

The Art Veneers Co. Ltd.
Industrial Estate
Mildenhall
Suffolk IP28 7AY
Tel: 0638 712550
Veneers, marquetry motifs, bandings,
period brassware.

The Bamboo People
Godmanstone
Dorchester
Dorset DTZ 7AF
Tel: 030 03 393
Cane and bamboo.

J. D. Beardmore & Co. Ltd.
3 Percy Street
London W1P 0EJ
Tel: 01 637 7041
and at:
49 Park Street
Bristol BS1 5NT
and
120 Western Road
Hove
Sussex BN3 1DB
Extensive range of reproduction cabinet
fittings in brass and other materials.

J. Crispin & Sons
92 Curtain Road
London EC2A 3AA
Tel: 01 739 4857
Veneers, inlay bandings, marquetry, motifs.

General Woodwork Supplies
76 Stoke Newington High Street
London N16 5BR
Tel: 01 254 6052
Hardwoods, including mouldings; turnery and
twistwork undertaken; brassware.

The Eaton Bag Co. Ltd.
16 Manette Street
London W1V 5LB
Tel: 01 437 9391
No catalogue as such: send sae for details
and samples. Woven grass matting and other
materials for table covering; rattan, bamboo
and split rattan for edging; raffia and cane.

Rustins Ltd.
Waterloo Road
London NW2
Tel: 01 450 4666
Comprehensive range of wood finishing and
restoring products.

Woodfit Ltd.
Whittle Low Mill
Chorley
Lancs PR6 7HB
Tel: 02572 66421
Furniture and cabinet fittings of all descriptions,
including some period knobs and handles.

Dryad Handicrafts
PO Box 38
Northgates
Leicester
Tel: 0533 50405
Wood graining comb.

T A Hutchinson Ltd.
16 St John's Lane
London EC1
Tel: 01 253 7769
Metal polishing materials.

A Bell & Co. Ltd.
Kingsthorpe Works
Northampton
NN2 6LT
Stone cleaning materials.

J. H. Ratcliffe & Co.
135a Linaker Street
Southport
Lancs
Tel: 0704 37999
Scumble.

Gedge & Co.
88 St. John Street
Clerkenwell
London EC1
Tel: 01 253 6057
Woodfiller, shellac, etc.

Lorant Engineers Ltd.
62 Southwark Bridge Road
London SE1 0AG
Tel: 01 928 8253
Hammerite.

John Heathcoat & Co. Ltd.
54 Great Marlborough Street
London W1
Tel: 01 437 9898
Soft net for mounting old, frail fabrics.

Yarncraft
Lodge Enterprises
112A Westbourne Grove
London W2
Tel: 01 229 1432
Extensive range of materials for tapestries and needlecraft

Coates
Needle Industries Ltd.
12 Seedhill Road
Paisley PA1 1JT
Tel: 041 887 9171

MacCulloch & Wallis
25 Dering Street
London W1
Tel: 01 629 0311
Fabric interlinings, pins, etc.

Russell Trading Co.
75 Paradise Street
Liverpool
Tel: 051 709 5752
Upholstery supplies

Whilst every effort is made to ensure that the addresses are correct at the time of going to press, readers are advised to check that suppliers have not moved before sending an order.

Index

Acetone 51, 54, 55, 56
adhesives 13, 15, 16, 20–21, 53,
    54

Bamboo furniture 29
beadwork 41, 42, 43
bran wash 42, 44, 47
brass 61, 63–5
Britannia metal 61, 66–7
burn marks 10, 22
button polish 24

Cane furniture 29–32
carpets and rugs 45
carvings 7, 8, 11, 21, 22 25
castors 18
caustic soda 22, 66
cellulose lacquer 9, 26
chairs 7, 15, 29–32, 33–9
chemical strippers 21–2, 23
chenille 44, 49
chinaware 51–7
    care and cleaning 51
    repairs to 21, 51–7
    stains on 51, 55
chintz 41, 44, 47
chromium plate 67
cold cure lacquer 24, 26
contact adhesives 21
copper 61, 63, 65
cotton 41, 44, 46, 47, 48, 49
cramping 14, 16
cretonne 44, 47
crewel work 47

Dovetail joints, 15, 16, 19
dowel joints 15, 16, 17
drawers 7, 14, 16, 19
dry cleaning 42, 44, 45, 46, 49
dyeing fabrics 41, 45, 49

Elm wood 9
embroidery 41, 42, 43, 46, 48
epoxy resin adhesives 21, 53–4,
    57, 59, 66, 74

Fabrics 41–9
    cleaning 41–2
    metallic threads in 42, 47
    repairs to 41, 48
    stain removal 47
    storage and display 42–4
    washing 42, 44, 45, 46, 47, 49
fray preventative 44, 45
French polish 8, 9, 10, 24–6

G-clamp 14
glassware 53, 58–9
glue film 21
gold 61–2
grain filler 23

Hallmarks 61, 62, 63
handles on furniture 7, 8, 17
hardwood 23
hinges 18–19
hydrogen peroxide 46, 54

Inlay 7, 8, 12–13

Joints, in woodwork 11, 15–16, 21

Kaolin powder 57
knobs, on furniture 8, 17

Lace 42, 43, 44, 46, 48, 49
leaf tables 19, 20
legs, furniture 20, 21, 22
linen 42, 46, 47
linseed oil 8, 9, 25, 27

Mahogany 24
marble 73, 75
marquetry 12, 21
metal fittings 8, 22, 64
metals 61–7
    cleaning 62–7
    hallmarks 61, 62, 63
    repairs to 62, 63, 65, 66
methylated spirit 10, 25, 49, 51,
    55, 56, 67

moiré silk 41, 45
moquette 41, 49
mortise and tenon joint 15, 16, 17
mouldings 7, 8, 11, 16, 21, 22, 25

Oil paintings 70
oiling wood 9, 24, 27
oxalic acid 47, 64, 66

Painted furniture 8, 23, 24, 26–7
patchwork quilts 42, 44
petit point 41, 42
pewter 61, 65–6
pictures, picture frames 69–71
pine 21, 24
polyurethane varnish 9, 24, 26
polyvinyl acetate (PVA) 16, 20, 21

Repair plates 15–16

Sanding 22, 23, 27
Scotch glue 15, 20
scraping wood 22, 23
shave hooks 23
silicone solution 73, 74
silk 44, 45, 46, 48, 49
silver 61, 62–3, 65
silver plate 61, 63
slate 76
soap jelly 42, 46, 47
splits in wood 11, 14, 16, 18
staining wood 23–4
stainless steel 67
stains, removal of
    on china 51, 55
    on fabrics 47
    on furniture 11
    on glassware 59
    on marble 75
stonework 73–4
Super-glue 21

Table leaves 7, 19–20
tapestry 41, 42, 43, 45
teak 9

teak oil 27
textiles see fabrics
turpentine 8, 64

Upholstery 33–9
    care of 42, 43, 47, 49
    drop in seats 33–6
    materials and tools for 33
    sprung seats 38–9
    unsprung seats 36–8
urea formaldehyde 21

Varnish 24, 70, 71, 76
velvet 41, 44, 49
veneers 8, 12–13, 14, 17, 21, 22

Watercolour paintings 69
wax polish 9
wax solvent 8
white polish 24
white spirit 8, 9, 64
whitewood 23, 24
wicker furniture 29
wood filler 11, 23
wood furniture 7–27
    cleaning 7, 8
    refinishing 7, 21–7
    repairs to 7, 8, 12–20, 21
    replacing parts 16–17
    reviving 8
    surface defects 8, 9, 10–11, 23
wool 42, 45, 46

Yew 9